AF226001

Writer in the court

Rudolph Kass (June 28, 1930 – June 4, 2021)
Associate Justice, Massachusetts Appeals Court (1979-2000)
Recall Justice (2000-2003)

Writer in the court

*Wit and wisdom in the decisions of
Justice Rudolph Kass of the
Massachusetts Appeals Court*

John Achatz

Boston
2023

To Rudy Kass,
a brilliant writer
and
a mentor to many.

Contents

<u>About Rudy</u>

<u>Cases</u>

CONTENTS

<u>Other writings</u>

PREFACE

Twenty years after Justice Rudolph Kass of the Massachusetts Appeals Court — I'll call him Rudy: everyone did — stepped down from the bench, people still talk about his judicial opinions, not so much because they established binding legal precedent (which, of course, they did), but because they are enjoyable to read.

On the occasion of the dedication of The Kass Library in the Kurlat Building in Brighton, it is fitting that the library have a collection of his writing. This slim volume collects a few of his most frequently-remembered decisions, and several articles from his student days and after retirement.

For a reader who might be daunted by the idea of reading legal text, the first few pages of this volume have snippets that are delightful to read on their own and show off Rudy's style. The full texts are included later.

Rudy loved words and writing. He knew that well-crafted humor can expose truth more plainly than paragraphs of explanatory prose.[1]

A biographical note

This is a collection of Rudy's writing[2], not a biography or memorial. Nonetheless, some basic biographical information is in order.

Rudolph Kass was born in Magdeburg, Germany on June 28, 1930, the second son of Heinrich Kass and Lily Mina Cohen, and died in Newton, Massachusetts on June 4, 2021, age 90.

While Rudy was a child, his family left Germany for safety, first in Tel Aviv, then New York, and finally in Lawrence. He graduated from Harvard, Class of '52, where he was a star writer and editor for the Harvard Crimson.

---

[1] See, for example, the tobacco-chewing sheep in *Allen* v. *Batchelder*, a snippet at page 10, full text at page 51 of this volume.

[2] Excepting Chief Justice Mark Green's remembrance which addresses the significance of Rudy's judicial writing.

After Harvard, he pursued journalism. Famously, while on assignment in Soviet-controlled East Berlin, he was arrested as a spy.[3]

After a year as a journalist, Rudy decided that a legal career would be better. He enrolled in Harvard Law School, graduating in 1956. He practiced law from 1956 until 1979 when he was appointed to the Appeals Court. His specialty was real estate law. He practiced in several firms, ultimately becoming a partner in Brown, Rudnick, Freed & Gesmer, which is where I met him. I was a young associate in the firm and Rudy was my supervisor.

Governor Michael Dukakis appointed Rudy to the Appeals Court. Rudy was sworn in in January 1979 and served until he reached the mandatory retirement age of 70 in 2000. He was recalled to the court to hear cases from 2000 until 2003 when he permanently retired from the court. Afterwards, he was a sought-after mediator in commercial disputes.

Rudy met Helen Kahn at a summer resort in Connecticut. She was a children's counselor and he was a beach boy. He often said this exposed him to the idea of discrimination based on gender. She worked harder than he did and was paid less. They married in 1953 and had three children, Elizabeth, Susan, and Peter.

Rudy served as counsel (often *pro bono*), member of the editorial board, or member of the board of directors of a staggering number of well-known publications and nonprofit organizations. Of special meaning today, Rudy was counsel to or a member of the board of his beloved Jewish Community Housing for the Elderly — now 2Life Communities — from its inception until his death.[4]

Acknowledgements

Many people helped and encouraged me in producing this volume. I acknowledge especially Brian Harkins at the Social Law Library for

---

[3] He was soon released.

[4] Much more has been written about Rudy and about his involvement with Brigham and Women's Hospital, Lawyers Weekly, Massachusetts Law Review, Boston Shakespeare Company, Ford Hall Forum, and on and on. An internet search will turn up many articles. I recommend the Boston Globe obituary, "Rudolph Kass, judge whose writing flair illuminated legal principles, dies at 90" by Bryan Marquard, June 13, 2021. The Boston Globe currently charges for access to its archives, but free access is often available at public libraries.

enthusiastic assistance in tracking down materials; Amy Schottenfels who spotted infelicities in the rough draft — any rough spots that remain are mine; and Chief Justice Mark Green who concurred in the decision of the Boston Bar Journal to allow me to reprint his remembrance.

JOHN ACHATZ
Boston
May 19, 2023

Snippets

WHAT IS A DELICATESSEN?

At the center of this case is the interpretation of a noncompetition clause in a lease: "Landlord will not permit the operation of any other delis in the Building during the term of this Lease."

...

If, as counsel for landlord suggested at oral argument, this case is about "what is a deli," a purist[1] would answer that a deli is a purveyor of central European delicacies such as corned beef, pastrami, brisket, chopped liver, lox, herring, whitefish, cream cheese, sour cream, sour pickles, pickled tongue, knockwurst, potato salad, cole slaw, and borscht.

Language, however, is a study in evolution, and the menu of the tenant, which initially did business as "O! Deli," offered considerably different attractions: butter croissant, tuna salad sandwiches, "Teriyaki Breast O! Chicken," yogurt, and — by way of saving grace — hot pastrami. The issue, as the O! Deli menu illuminates, is not what, as matter of law, constitutes a deli. Rather, the issue is: what did the parties mean by deli in their noncompetition clause?

Kobayashi v. *Orion Ventures*, 42 Mass. App. Ct. 492 (1997)

Full text at page 31.

---

[1] That purist, however, would be mistaken. According to Joan Nathan in Jewish Cooking in America 184-186 (1994), the first delicatessens in America "were primarily run by Germans and Alsatians." They served kuchen (cake), kraut (cabbage), fish, bread and wurst (sausage). "The word [delicatessen] itself derives from German and means delicacies, but is used not only to describe a shop but is also the word for the products sold in a shop. Eventually, Jews, too, went into the business," and the offerings began to take on the character described in the main text. According to Ms. Nathan and other authorities, a quintessential deli was the Carnegie in New York, whose proprietor said after a robbery, "Idiots! They took the money and left the pastrami."

SOMETIMES A DOG'S BARK

Sometimes a dog's bark can be as bad as its bite. Thus, [the statute] authorizes selectmen of a town to determine that a dog "is a nuisance by reason of ... excessive barking" and to "make such order concerning ... the disposal of such dog as may be deemed necessary." The selectmen of Phillipston issued an order on April 5, 1993, directing the defendant Buzzell, a breeder of dogs, to remove his dogs because they barked too much. [...] Three years later, in 1996, dogs were still on Buzzell's premises — and barking. [...][T]he Commonwealth brought proceedings against Buzzell charging him with sixteen violations of the dog removal order. The Commonwealth's complaint was tried in District Court to a jury of six, which returned verdicts of guilty[.]

 ...

Buzzell's principal claim of error is that [...] the Commonwealth had failed to prove that at least one of the dogs present on the defendant's property on the date of the removal order, April 5, 1993, was still present and barking during the period, March, 1996, through September, 1996, that the sixteen counts in the complaint encompass. One might have thought that point disposed of in [...] a similar case, in which we wrote, "It was not incumbent upon the Commonwealth to show that the dogs in the defendant's possession on the dates of the complaints were identical in being and number to the dogs which were the subject of the removal order." [...] The mischief to be corrected is excessive barking and whether the source of the barking on the premises is Fang or Fido is not of the essence. Had the defendant kept a quiet dog on his premises after the removal order, the case might stand differently.

Commonwealth v. *Buzzell*, 49 Mass. App. Ct. 902 (2000)

Full text at page 45.

WOLF DOING WHAT CARNIVORES DO

A wolf in the New Bedford Buttonwood Park Zoo, a city facility, pushed enough of his snout through his pen to bite the plaintiff's finger. This action against the superintendent of parks of New Bedford alleged negligence in permitting the existence of a pen from which a wolf, doing what carnivores will, could bite someone on the viewing side of the enclosure.

Alfonso v. Lowney, 11 Mass. App. Ct. 338 (1981)

Full text at page 47.

TOBACCO-CHEWING SHEEP

Sebastian, the tobacco-chewing sheep, would have been disconcerted by this appeal. His status as a Martha's Vineyard tourist attraction was a function of his visibility on the Allen farm, astride the South Road in Chilmark.

Sebastian could not have achieved the modest notoriety he enjoyed without tenure of the Allen farm by his owners, Henry and Maude Allen. The appellant, Batchelder, has called in question the exclusivity of the Allens' title, which has come down to Clarissa Allen (Clarissa). [...] In light of 150 years of well developed case law, we conclude that the appellant's position is so untenable as to be frivolous.

...

After a long trial, the Land Court judge found that, at least from 1892, "the Allen farm was possessed by various members of the Allen family to the exclusion of any cotenant in common." Clarissa's grandfather, Henry Allen, was well known in Chilmark. He held office as selectman, assessor, overseer of the poor and town moderator, manifesting a bent for public life which a witness, Captain Poole, attributed to Henry's being "lazier than hell ... he was a typical small-town politician. He'd pat you on the back wherever you met him and agree with you 100 percent."

Allen v. *Batchelder*, 17 Mass. App. Ct. 453 (1984)

Full text at page 51.

Hug before they marry

Once again we consider in what circumstances a writing, which by context or by terms contemplates a more formal agreement, may nonetheless serve as a binding contract.

...

Under a caption which read, "PURCHASE AND SALE," there appeared the following sentence: "A mutually acceptable Purchase and Sale Agreement shall be executed within four weeks of acceptance of this offer."

Before a purchase and sale agreement was signed, [defendant] received an offer to buy its property that was $78,000 higher than that which [plaintiff] had made. [Defendant] became inattentive to calls from [plaintiff] or the broker.

...

On the basis of the judge's findings, for which there is support in the record, that the preliminary agreement covered all material points and that the parties so regarded it, the case falls into that category where execution of a more formal instrument "was hardly more than a formality."

...

This is not to say that parties to a preliminary agreement may not provide that they do not intend to be bound until the transaction is buttoned up by a more detailed and formal agreement. There is commercial utility to allowing persons to hug before they marry.

Goren v. *Royal Investments*, 25 Mass. App. Ct. 137 (1987)

Full text at page 59.

DINING MIGHT BE AN INFLATED TERM

What Atlantic Richfield Oil Company and Howard Johnson Company had in mind in 1971, when Atlantic Richfield imposed a use restriction on its land along State Route 15, was simple enough. Atlantic Richfield would sell gas and Howard Johnson would sell food.

…

[Howard Johnson was replaced by] two franchise restaurants, a "Roy Rogers" and a "Sbarro." Both provided for on-the-premises eating (dining might be an inflated term).

…

Mobil[, Atlantic Richfield's successor,] in 1994 was distinctively expansive. The whole layout in the customer area of the gas station was altered to emphasize food sales.

…

It requires no leap of the imagination to understand that to the extent carry-out food more substantial than a candy bar or package of crackers was conveniently available where customers paid for gas, some of those customers would buy something to eat then and there and would be lost as food customers by Roy Rogers and Sbarro. Conversely, customers limited to a choice of peanut crackers and a can of Pepsi-Cola were more likely to opt for the heady delights of the restaurants next door.

Exit 1 Properties Ltd. Partnership v. *Mobil Oil Corp.*, 44 Mass. App. Ct. 571 (1998)

Full text at page 65.

LEVEL OF RASCALITY THAT WOULD
RAISE AN EYEBROW

Although the underlying cause is a contract action for material sold and services delivered, the insertion in the complaint of a claim under [consumer protection law], requires consideration once again of the reach of that statutory provision to commercial disputes between business organizations.

...

It remains to ask whether, on the facts found, Forbes has committed a transgression which exposes it to a c. 93A claim, i.e., did it do anything unfair or deceptive? What is unfair is a definitional problem of long standing, which statutory draftsmen have prudently avoided. "It is impossible to frame definitions which embrace all unfair practices. There is no limit to human inventiveness in this field." H.R. Conf. Rep. No. 1142, 63d Cong., 2d Sess. (1914). The criteria adopted in our decisions [...] require us in a case such as this to look for conduct which is (1) within "at least the penumbra of some common-law, statutory, or other established concept of unfairness; (2) [...] is immoral, unethical, oppressive, or unscrupulous ..." Whether a given practice runs afoul of these touchstones must be determined from the circumstances of each case. The objectionable conduct must attain a level of rascality that would raise an eyebrow of someone inured to the rough and tumble of the world of commerce.

Levings v. *Forbes & Wallace, Inc.,* 8 Mass. App. Ct. 498 (1979)

Full text at page 71.

FEW EVENTS SO STIR THE CIVIC CONSCIOUSNESS AS THE REMOVAL OF CONVENIENT PARKING

In 1977, Marshfield, acting through its department of public works, was on the brink of constructing a wastewater treatment plant and appurtenant sewage pumping stations. [Abutters appealed the issuance of a permit for the pumping station. As part of settlement, the city agreed not to allow parking on nearby land.]

...

The following summer there were several inconclusive procedural maneuvers [in litigation seeking to overturn a parking restriction related to the project] which it is not necessary to detail, except to observe that they were stimulated by residents of the town aggrieved by the loss of parking which they were accustomed to have available when visiting Green Harbor Beach. Few events so stir the civic consciousness as the removal of convenient parking.

Bowers v. *Board of Appeals of Marshfield*, 16 Mass. App. Ct. 29 (1983)

Full text at page 79.

Making a sail out of a hog's ear

Before the developer made it the site of a condominium, Spinnaker Island was known as Hog Island, a less tony address. The developer made a sail out of a hog's ear.

> *Spinnaker Island & Yacht* v. *Board of Assessors of Hull*, 49 Mass. App. Ct. 20 (2000)

> Full text at page 85.

THEFT OF A CHOCOLATE COOKIE RECIPE: THE DEFENDANT'S ARGUMENT CRUMBLES

Nothing is sacred. We have before us a case of theft of a recipe for baking chocolate chip cookies.

…

The judge found that, from the beginning of its use, Kitchens carefully guarded the cookie recipe. One copy of the recipe was locked in an office safe. A duplicate was secured in the desk of William Wolf, Lawton's son. […] For work day use, […] access to the [recipe] was limited to long-time trusted employees [including Hogan].

…

Hogan and his wife organized a bakery business to sell prepackaged bakery products under the trade name Hogie Bear. Among the first products Hogie Bear made was a chocolate chip cookie. […] The judge found Hogie Bear's cookie "similar in appearance, color, cell construction, texture, flavor and taste.[1]

…

Hogan's argument crumbles.

Peggy Lawton Kitchens v. *Terence M. Hogan* , 18 Mass. App. Ct. 937 (1984)

Full text at page 91.

---

[1] Samples were served up as part of the record on appeal. The time consumed by the appellate process caused the cookies to be in a condition which rendered an appellate taste test of dubious utility, if not downright dangerous.

Saint Joan

One playwright after another has taken a whack at writing a play about Joan of Arc but the play by Bernard Shaw currently being produced at the Plymouth is the pick of the basket. Perhaps its appeal lies in that it avoids being a tearjerker, the fault of several Joan plays, and instead works on the emotions in an honest way.

Much of "Saint Joan" is like much of Shaw: lectures amusingly presented in dialogue form. Yet on several occasions he comes up with lines so thrilling, so poetic, that one starts to consider his claims against his self-chosen arch rival in literary history — Shakespeare.

The Harvard Crimson, September 25, 2951

Full text at page 97.

Brass Tacks: The campaign

The McCarran Act: A Test

During the current congressional campaign scarcely a candidate has neglected an opportunity to accuse his opponent of knowingly or unknowingly lending aid and comfort to the Communists. The Korean War has so increased the sensitivity of United States public opinion to the threat of Communism, the politicians think, that fierce opposition to it will be a better political asset than an admirable home life and advocacy of virtue.

Support or opposition to the McCarran Anti-Communist Law has often been used as a measure of anti-Communist feeling. The few outspoken enemies of the law who are up for office — Helen Gahagen Douglas of California, John Carroll of Colorado, Jacob Javitts of New York, and Herbert Lehman of New York — claim that the McCarran Act has so many weaknesses that it will do the Communists more good than harm. Backers of the Act assert that to oppose it implies weak tolerance of the Communists if not outright sympathy with them.

. . .

It is the law which nobody wants, yet it passed through the Senate and over a presidential veto by a vote of 77 to 7, one of the largest margins by which a measure has been approved in the Senate, other than a declaration of war.

It passed so easily because the senators thought it would be political suicide to vote against anti-Communist legislation. So strong was this feeling that Hubert Humphrey of [Minnesota] voted for the McCarran bill 24 hours after he said on the Senate floor that "the day S. 4037 passes will prove to be one of the darkest pages in American History."

. . .

If some of the anti-McCarran Act campaigners win, it may convince politicians that voting against anti-Communist legislation isn't suicide. Repeal or drastic amendment of the current law may then become a possibility. If many opponents of the McCarran Act lose, especially so strong a figure as Lehman, the Act will probably remain unchanged.

The Harvard Crimson, November 2, 1950

Full text at page 99.

MEDIATION THEATER

"How many ages hence shall this our lofty scene be acted over in states unborn and accents yet unknown."[2]

Consider these scenes from mediation theater:

[Rudy sketches scenes from three plots.]

What is acted over in these three scenes, is personal anger: (1) condominium owners living with construction defects 24 hours a day; (2) neighbors at war over a boundary line; and (3) a human resources manager who did her job as she saw it and yet angered management by her contumacious ignoring senior management order.

In disputes between commercial consenting adults, there will certainly be some theater, several hours of it, but thereafter each party will begin to make risk assessments: the likely litigation expenses and the paralyzing effect on each of the parties if the dispute is allowed to fester.

The Mediation Group blog, June 6, 2016

Full text at page 101.

---

[2] Shakespeare, Julius Caesar, Act III, Scene 1

About Rudy

HON. RUDOLPH KASS
(in his own words)

Access to Justice Fellow (2017-2018) biography
https://lawyersclearinghouse.org/hon-rudolph-kass/

From January 1979 to September 2003, the Honorable Rudolph Kass served as an Associate Justice of the Massachusetts Appeals Court. During his tenure, he was the author of 1,680 opinions of the court as well as approximately 200 single justice memoranda and orders.

Prior to his appointment to the court, he was a partner in the Boston law firm Brown, Rudnick, Freed & Gesmer (now Brown Rudnick). His area of specialty was real estate, concentrating in urban affairs, i.e., urban renewal projects and government assisted housing, zoning, land use planning law, real estate financing, eminent domain and taxation. He was on the drafting committee that wrote the Massachusetts condominium law and was an active practitioner in that area. As counsel to the 1965 special legislative commission on low-income housing, he was a principal draftsman of the statute that created the Massachusetts Housing Finance Agency.

During the period between his retirement in June 2000 from the Appeals Court at the constitutionally mandated age, and before being recalled for additional service on the court, he acted as a mediator and arbitrator. He chaired an advisory committee to the Supreme Judicial Court concerning electronic access to trial court records. In addition, he chaired an advisory board to the Governor on ferry service to Martha's Vineyard and Nantucket. He also acted as an expert on Massachusetts law for the United States State Department in an arbitration under the North American Free Trade Agreement. Judge Kass joined The Mediation Group in 2003, resolving disputes over real estate, contracts, insurance coverage issues and a range of other civil matters.

Judge Kass has been involved in numerous community

organizations, including the Cambridge Center for Adult Education, Jewish Community Housing for the Elderly (JCHE)[1], the Ford Hall Forum, Brigham and Women's Hospital and Greater Boston Legal Services. He is a member of the Supreme Judicial Court Judiciary/Media Committee. Judge Kass has taught a real estate course built around commercial leases as an adjunct professor of law at Boston College Law School, as well as edited and authored publications for Massachusetts Continuing Legal Education, Inc. He is a member of the editorial board of the Massachusetts Law Review and a member of the advisory editorial board of Massachusetts Lawyers Weekly.

As an Access to Justice Fellow, Judge Kass will continue to work with **Greater Boston Legal Services** (GBLS), mentoring young lawyers. The GBLS mission is to provide free legal assistance to as many low-income families as possible to help them secure some of the most basic necessities of life.

---

[1] Now 2Life Communities.

Personal Reflections on the Life and Legacy of Justice Rudolph Kass

Mark V. Green
Chief Justice, Massachusetts Appeals Court

Boston Bar Journal, November 3, 2021

Voice of the Judiciary

How can I attempt to capture the legacy of my good friend and former colleague, Justice Rudy Kass? It is a daunting assignment: to offer words on behalf of one of the most colorful and talented wordsmiths ever to serve on a Massachusetts appellate court. Rather than try to use my words to do him justice, I will, for the most, part allow his words to speak for themselves, with a couple of personal memories added for good measure.

I first met Rudy Kass, and Helen, in the fall of 1997, as we took our seats in a shuttle bus from the airport in Great Falls, Montana to the hotel where our little group would stay before launching a canoe trip down the upper Missouri River, retracing a portion of the Lewis and Clark journey described in Steven Ambrose's Undaunted Courage. It was one in a series of back country excursions organized by Superior Court Judge Paul Chernoff and, just four months into my time as a trial judge in the Massachusetts Land Court, I was most fortunate to be included among four other veteran Superior Court judges, and Rudy. I was as nervous as a teenager at a high school dance, which is the only explanation I can offer for my ill-advised choice to initiate small talk by praising an opinion by Supreme Judicial Court Justice Charles Fried in the case of *Goulding* v. *Cook*. I did not know that Rudy had authored the Appeals Court opinion in the same case, and that Justice Fried's soaring rhetoric reversed the conclusion Rudy and the Appeals Court had expressed. It is a testament to Rudy's good nature and graciousness that, despite that awkward beginning, he took me under his wing and mentored me throughout my judicial career, and became a beloved friend.

My experience with Rudy was built principally around our work as judges. We bonded over a shared love of what we both called "dirt law." Real estate is always about location, and each location has its own story. With his background as a newsman, Rudy was particularly expert at seeing and telling those stories in ways that spoke to lawyers and lay readers alike, breaking down subtle and complex legal concepts into terms that anyone could understand. But he also invariably added a level of color often absent from appellate caselaw. I have my own list of favorites among his opinions, but there are many other contenders.

In *Allen* v. *Batchelder*, 17 Mass. App. Ct. 453 (1984) for example, he explained the concept of ouster — the doctrine by which one fractional owner of property may extinguish the interest of another — by telling the story from an unusual perspective, opening the opinion with the following unforgettable line: "Sebastian, the tobacco chewing sheep, would have been disconcerted by this appeal." He went on to explain how Sebastian symbolized the open and obvious — and longstanding — occupation the Allen family had made of the farm they claimed now to own, free of any fractional interest held by the distant heirs of a former cotenant.

In the field of real estate law in particular, Rudy was legendary. On the sometimes murky question of when parties became bound during their progression from an offer to purchase to full agreement, Rudy offered a simple and pragmatic, but also evocative, framework for the preliminary stages of negotiation in *Goren* v. *Royal Investments*, 25 Mass. App. Ct. 137 (1987): "There is commercial utility" he observed, "in allowing persons to hug before they marry."

On a question of interpretation of a noncompetition covenant in a lease, in *Kobayashi* v. *Orion Ventures*, 42 Mass. App. Ct. 492 (1997), he discussed the essential nature of a delicatessen, including a footnote recounting the classic comment by the proprietor of the Carnegie Deli in New York following a robbery: "Idiots! They took the money and left the pastrami!" By the way, should you be tempted to follow this lead to read the full opinion, I also commend to you footnote 9, which illustrates the circular logic of an argument by reference to Gilbert and Sullivan.

Rudy's style was such that his hand was obvious even in a brief rescript opinion, issued without authoring attribution. When I opened the daily advance sheets on the morning of April 25, 2000 and saw the opening line of *Commonwealth* v. *Buzzell*, 49 Mass. App. Ct. 902 (2000), I knew immediately who had written it. The case involved a challenge to the sufficiency of the evidence supporting conviction under a statute requiring removal of dogs whose barking caused a nuisance. The defendant argued that there was no proof that the dogs who provoked the complaint were the same as those who remained on his property on the date he was arrested for failing to remove them. Rudy's opinion opens as follows. "Sometimes a dog's bark can be as bad as its bite." Continuing, he explains that "The answer to the defendant's 'at least one identical dog' argument is that [the statute] recognizes the fungibility of barking dogs. The mischief to be corrected is excessive barking and whether the source of the barking on the premises is Fang or Fido is not of the essence." Rudy was surely one of the most visible members of the Appeals Court in its history, and remains one of those most often cited.

Rudy also was notable for his continuing engagement in the wider community. While the Code of Judicial Conduct does not prohibit judges from engaging in their communities, the limitations often cumulatively, over time, induce many long-serving judges to follow the path of least resistance and withdraw, at least somewhat. But not Rudy — he remained active in more social clubs than I knew to exist, and contributed generously on a wide variety of charitable boards. His visibility in our wider community was not merely a product of the prominence of his judicial writings.

As I came to know Rudy, I also came to know Helen. Theirs was an inspiring and continuing romance. It was evident in even the most casual observation of the two of them together — and they were almost always together — how intertwined they were. They demonstrated a comfortable and gentle intimacy, based on mutual respect, that was a model of what a marriage can be.

When I think of the attributes that most describe Rudy, three come to mind: optimism, curiosity, and adventurousness. Combined, the three capture his openness to new ideas, to new ways of doing things, and to new friends. He is an iconic figure in the Massachusetts judiciary, but his legacy extends beyond his work to the personal connection he made with so many. As a giant in the judiciary, and as a friend, he is greatly missed.

The Honorable Mark V. Green was appointed Chief Justice of the Appeals Court by Governor Charles D. Baker on December 6, 2017, having served on the Court as an Associate Justice since his appointment by Governor Jane M. Swift on November 1, 2001. He holds a Bachelor of Arts degree in philosophy from Cornell University, with distinction in all subjects, and is a 1982 cum laude graduate of Harvard Law School. He is a former member of the Board of Editors of the Boston Bar Journal.

Cases

Takaji Kobayashi & others, trustees,[1] *v.* Orion Ventures, Inc. (and a companion case[2])

42 Mass. App. Ct. 492

Suffolk. December 5, 1996 – April 18, 1997.

Present: Perretta, Kass, & Jacobs, JJ.

Civil Action commenced in the Superior Court Department on June 22, 1993.

Summary Process. Complaint filed in the Boston Municipal Court Department on September 19, 1994.

After consolidation for trial in the Superior Court, the cases were tried before *Margot Botsford*, J.

Michael R. Coppock (*David C. Fixler* with him) for Takaji Kobayashi & others.

Damian R. LaPlaca for Orion Ventures, Inc.

Kass, J.

At the center of this case is the interpretation of a noncompetition clause in a lease: "Landlord will not permit the operation of any other delis in the Building during the term of this Lease." That pivotal phrase appeared in the last sentence of s. 4 of a commercial lease between the trustees of Shuwa Trust, as landlord, to Orion Ventures, Inc., as tenant, for space to be used by tenant as a restaurant.

If, as counsel for landlord suggested at oral argument, this case is about "what is a deli," a purist[3] would answer that a deli is a purveyor

---

[1] Yoshio Yamashita and Takeshi Shiratori, all as trustees of Shuwa Trust of Boston.

[2] *Orion Ventures, Inc. vs. Takaji Kobayashi & others, trustees.*

[3] That purist, however, would be mistaken. According to Joan Nathan in Jewish Cooking in America 184-186 (1994), the first delicatessens in America "were primarily run by Germans and Alsatians." They served kuchen (cake), kraut (cabbage), fish, bread and

of central European delicacies such as corned beef, pastrami, brisket, chopped liver, lox, herring, whitefish, cream cheese, sour cream, sour pickles, pickled tongue, knockwurst, potato salad, cole slaw, and borscht.

Language, however, is a study in evolution, and the menu of the tenant, which initially did business as "O! Deli," offered considerably different attractions: butter croissant, tuna salad sandwiches, "Teriyaki Breast O! Chicken," yogurt, and — by way of saving grace — hot pastrami. The issue, as the O! Deli menu illuminates, is not what, as matter of law, constitutes a deli. Rather, the issue is: what did the parties mean by deli in their noncompetition clause?

A jury decided that the landlord violated the noncompetition clause and assessed damages. The Superior Court judge who presided over the trial ruled that the landlord's violation of the noncompetition clause did not constitute an unfair practice within the meaning of G. L. c. 93A. In a companion summary process case that had been consolidated for trial, the judge awarded judgment of possession to the landlord and assessed damages against the tenant. Both sides have appealed. We affirm the judgments.

These are the facts of the dispute, as the jury might have found them on the evidence most favorable to the plaintiff in each case. Following several months of negotiation, the landlord and tenant on October 28, 1987, executed a lease for 1,120 square feet on the ground floor of 265 Franklin Street in Boston. The tenant described to the landlord the sort of fast-food breakfast and lunch establishment that it proposed to operate, the importance of employees of office tenants in the same building as potential customers, and the need, therefore, for some protection from competitors dishing out similar food. That concern led to the "[no] other delis in the Building" clause.

The tenant opened for business (as O! Deli) in October, 1988. Its breakfast fare ("Morning Starters"), sold between 6 and 11 A.M., offered

---

wurst (sausage). "The word [delicatessen] itself derives from German and means delicacies, but is used not only to describe a shop but is also the word for the products sold in a shop. Eventually, Jews, too, went into the business," and the offerings began to take on the character described in the main text. According to Ms. Nathan and other authorities, a quintessential deli was the Carnegie in New York, whose proprietor said after a robbery, "Idiots! They took the money and left the pastrami."

"Egg O! Muffin," assorted muffins, croissants, bagels, coffee, tea, and a variety of juices. Lunch business was heaviest in sandwiches and beverages. The tenant achieved a net profit of approximately $70,000 in 1989 and $65,000 in 1990. In 1991, a high vacancy rate at 265 Franklin Street and general economic decline combined to take net profits down to $10,000.

Throughout this period, Brandy Pete's, a more formal sitdown restaurant also operated off, and open to, the lobby of 265 Franklin Street. The tenant did not regard Brandy Pete's as competition because it catered to a slow-food patron. In April, 1992, Brandy Pete's subleased a portion of its space to a cart that from 6 A.M. to 3 P.M. sold pastries, muffins, scones, bagels, as well as coffee, gourmet coffees (flavored), espresso, cappuccino, and cafe latte. By mid-1992, tenant began to feel the effect of the cart's — which called itself Caffe Presto — morning competition.[4]

Starting in March, 1993, Jay White, the principal of the tenant, proposed a variety of rent reductions to compensate for the loss of business that White thought to be caused by the Caffe Presto cart. He also asked the landlord's consent to convert the tenant's operation to a Burger King. The landlord offered no succor; rather, it reminded the tenant on May, 1993, that under the lease the base rent was rising from $4,200 per month to $4,523 per month.

The tenant was first at the bar with a complaint asking for a declaratory judgment (that under the lease it was entitled to protection from the landlord against Caffe Presto); injunctive relief against Caffe Presto; damages for breach of contract (the noncompetition clause); and unfair and deceptive practices within the meaning of G. L. c. 93A, s. 11. The landlord counterclaimed that the tenant's complaint was not only manifestly without foundation in law but was an abuse of process, the tenant's ulterior and sole motive for the action being to obtain a decrease in rent under its lease. Some six months after filing its complaint, the tenant stopped paying rent. The landlord responded with a summary process action in Boston Municipal Court. The two matters were

---

[4] In November of 1992, O! Deli changed its name to Ernie's Cafe. The gastronomic formula remained the same.

consolidated for trial in Superior Court.[5]

1. The meaning of the noncompetition clause. The landlord's first point on appeal is that the parol evidence rule was a bar to considering testimony from White, who, it will be recalled, was the tenant's principal officer, and from the tenant's lawyer. Both were allowed to testify about what was said in negotiations about the noncompetition clause. According to the landlord, the trial judge erred in allowing the jury to consider that testimony. White was allowed to testify that he presented a copy of the O! Deli menu to Ed Daley, who was negotiating for the landlord, that he told Daley he did not want competition for that kind of restaurant business in the building, and that Daley had "understood the intent of what was wanted." The tenant's lawyer testified that Daley agreed to the "concept" of prohibiting any competitor from selling items in the building similar to those sold by the tenant. That testimony was not objected to but, because the parol evidence rule is one of substantive law, *Scirpo* v. *McMillan*, 355 Mass. 657, 661 (1969), the landlord is not barred from arguing that prior conversations should not have been considered to vary the terms of an unambiguous, integrated written instrument.

The judge correctly ruled that, notwithstanding an "integration clause" in the lease[6] declaring that no prior oral statements were to have any effect, the lease was profoundly ambiguous about the meaning of "[n]o other delis." To that degree the instrument was not fully integrated. Evidence was needed to shed light on what the parties had in mind when they used the term "deli." See *New England Fin. Resources, Inc.* v. *Coulouras*, 30 Mass. App. Ct. 140, 146-147 (1991). The parol evidence rule only bars the introduction of prior or contemporaneous written or oral agreements that contradict, vary, or broaden an integrated writing. *Gifford* v. *Gifford*, 354 Mass. 247, 249 (1968). *Hogan* v.

---

[5] By the time the case had come to trial, the tenant had abandoned the leased space. The declaratory judgment and injunctive relief counts in the tenant's complaint had become moot and, as such, were dismissed. The portion of the summary process case that was not mooted was the tenant's liability for rent.

[6] Section 33 of the lease provided as follows: "This Lease contains the entire and only agreement between the parties, and no oral statements or representations or prior written matter not contained or referred to in this instrument shall have any force or effect. This Lease shall not be modified in any way except by a writing subscribed by the parties hereto."

Riemer, 35 Mass. App. Ct. 360, 364-365 (1993). Restatement (Second) of Contracts s. 215 (1981). It does not bar extrinsic evidence that elucidates the meaning of an ambiguous contract term. *Robert Indus., Inc.* v. *Spence*, 362 Mass. 751, 753-754 (1973). *Vezina* v. *Mahoney & Wright Ins. Agency, Inc.*, 40 Mass. App. Ct. 218, 223 (1996). Restatement (Second) of Contracts s. 214(c) comment b. See also *USM Corp.* v. *Arthur D. Little Sys., Inc.*, 28 Mass. App. Ct. 108, 116 (1989); *Parrish* v. *Parrish*, 30 Mass. App. Ct. 78, 86 (1991).

"Deli" was not defined in the lease; nor was it self-defining. Compare *New England Fin. Resources, Inc.* v. *Coulouras*, 30 Mass. App. Ct. at 146-147, and *Vezina* v. *Mahoney & Wright Ins. Agency, Inc.*, 40 Mass. App. Ct. at 223, with *Ober* v. *National Cas. Co.*, 318 Mass. 27, 29-30 (1945), and *Jefferson Ins. Co.* v. *Holyoke*, 23 Mass. App. Ct. 472, 474-475 (1987). The tenant, whose lawyer concocted the "[n]o other delis" language, presumably had in mind an establishment that served out food of the sort on the tenant's O! Deli menu, a definition that another person, but not necessarily the landlord, might have thought a degradation of language.

The landlord complains that the evidence received on behalf of the tenant stripped the word "deli" of all meaning; it came to signify selling food in a manner, i.e., over the counter, similar to that purveyed by the tenant. Put another way, the sale of any line of food and drink that competed with the tenant's operation became a "deli." From the tenant's view that is precisely right. The answer to the landlord's protest is that, once parties use a word as chameleonic as "deli," the finder of fact — here the jury — may extract the intended meaning of "deli," for purposes of the document, from the circumstances that led to its use. The object of the inquiry was "to ascertain the meaning intended to be attached to the words by the parties who used them ...." *Clark* v. *State St. Trust Co.*, 270 Mass. 140, 151-152 (1930). See *Hubert* v. *Melrose-Wakefield Hosp. Assn.*, 40 Mass. App. Ct. 172, 177 (1996).

2. *Evidentiary exclusions.* a. *Evidence under the doctrine of verbal completeness.* The tenant, without objection from the landlord, placed in evidence several of the landlord's internal memoranda. One was from Yoshio Yamashita, a trustee of the landlord, putting to Stephen Howard, the manager of the 265 Franklin Street building, some questions about the landlord's legal position in connection with the Caffe Presto

operation; the other was Howard's two-page, typewritten response to those questions. From those documents the tenant's counsel read to the jury selectively, leaving the impression (taking a view of the evidence favorable to the plaintiff-tenant) that, contemporaneously with those memoranda, agents of the landlord were conscious of a violation of the noncompetition clause. On redirect examination, the landlord's counsel asked Howard to read other parts of his memo, notably: "The Caffe Presto operation I feel does not fit the description as a deli and I also feel that [tenant] is using this lease clause to negotiate a reduction in rent."

The trial judge sustained an objection.

Under the rule of verbal completeness, when a party places in evidence part of what was said or written at a particular time, the other party may add what has been omitted to give a full picture. *Commonwealth* v. *Watson*, 377 Mass. 814, 825-831 (1979). *Evans* v. *Multicon Constr. Corp.*, 30 Mass. App. Ct. 728, 741 (1991); Liacos, Massachusetts Evidence s. 3.12 (6th ed. 1994). That principle does not open the gate for everything in a document or statement. There is always the test of relevance. Ibid. Here, the excluded material served to rebut an impression (of an admission of consciousness of violation of the noncompetition clause) that might have been formed by the jury from the parts of the Howard memorandum that had previously been read. Those of Howard's reflections that the tenant's counsel had elided should have been admitted under the rule of verbal completeness.

The error was inconsequential, however, because Howard was later allowed to testify directly that he thought Caffe Presto was not conducting a deli operation.[7] Moreover, the written memorandum itself was taken in evidence, and the jury, therefore, had the entire document to consider. The inability of the landlord's counsel to read aloud the lines in the indented paragraph above could not have made a material difference. See *DeJesus* v. *Yogel*, 404 Mass. 44, 48-49 (1989).

b. Dictionary definitions. Another category of exclusion that the landlord presses as erroneous was the trial judge's refusal to receive photocopies of definitions of "deli" and "delicatessen" from four authoritative English language dictionaries. Those definitions had

---

[7] Howard's testimony in this regard was received in connection with the tenant's c. 93A claim, but he spoke in the presence of the jury without limiting instruction.

something to say about the common understanding of the word "deli" and were probative, the landlord suggests, of what the parties intended. It would not have been error to receive the proffered photocopies, but, equally, the judge could be forgiven for thinking that dictionary definitions had only marginal relevance to what was in the minds of businessmen and lawyers pragmatically hammering out a lease. The exclusion of the photocopies was within the judge's discretion. As it turned out, the judge, in her instructions, read to the jury a dictionary definition of "deli" and allowed the jurors to consider it.

3. *Measure of the tenant's damages.* After charging the jury generally about contract damages,[8] the judge broke the question into two parts. First, the jurors were to consider the damages the tenant had sustained from the date of the breach (a fact for the jury to find) to the termination of the lease on September 6, 1994 (a fact that the parties had stipulated). Second, the jurors were to assess damages that the tenant had sustained to the end of the ten-year term of the lease, i.e., through October 28, 1998. The jury found damages of $105,000 as to part one and $115,000 as to part two.

The landlord had requested the judge to instruct the jury that, as to part one, the calculation of damages should begin, not on the date when a breach of the noncompetition clause in the lease first occurred, but when the tenant first complained to the landlord that the Caffe Presto operation violated the "no other deli" provision. While a lease could provide that a landlord was not liable for damages until a breach had been called to its attention and it had an opportunity to cure it, the landlord has not staked its position on a lease clause but apparently on the not entirely irrational idea that the nature of the violation was such that a landlord would not be cognizant of it until complained of by a tenant. That proposition, however, is contrary to basic contract law, viz., that the measure of damages is the amount which places the injured party in as good a position as if the contract had been performed.

---

[8] The judge charged as follows: "[T]he injured party is entitled to be placed in the same position it would have been in if the contract had been performed .... In the context of a breach of a covenant or a provision of a lease, this principle of damages means that [tenant], as the party suffering the breach, if you find that, indeed, [tenant] did suffer a breach, is entitled to recover the difference between the value of the lease to [tenant] with the covenant against competition ... and the value of the lease interest to [tenant] with the covenant having been broken by having another deli in the building.

American Mechanical Corp. v. *Union Mach. Co. of Lynn*, 21 Mass. App. Ct. 97, 101 (1985). Restatement (Second) of Contracts s. 344, s. 347 comment a (1981). 5 Corbin, Contracts s. 992 (1964). Calculating damages as of the date of breach achieves that objective. Beginning to count damages for violation of a noncompetition clause only from the time of protest to the landlord would leave the tenant only partially compensated.

As to the second part of the damages question, the landlord asked the judge to instruct the jury that the tenant could not claim damages after the landlord had terminated the lease for nonpayment of rent. The landlord's theory was that the noncompetition clause applied during the term of the lease and could not be violated once the lease had ended. That sounds logical, but the logic is Gilbertian.[9] Its flaw is that, on the theory of the tenant's case, what caused the termination in the first place was the competition from Caffe Presto that the landlord had permitted and which so bled tenant that it could no longer pay the rent. Having, in that manner, brought about the termination, the landlord is responsible for the consequences. See Restatement (Second) of Contracts s. 352 comment a.

Those consequences may include such prospective profits as are susceptible of proof with a reasonable degree of certainty, yet short of mathematical exactness. *Lowrie* v. *Castle*, 225 Mass. 37, 51-52 (1916). *Augat, Inc.* v. *Aegis, Inc.*, 417 Mass. 484, 488 n.4. (1994). *Frank D. Wayne Assocs., Inc.* v. *Lussier*, 16 Mass. App. Ct. 986, 988 (1983). The tenant presented evidence of its monthly sales and net profits before and after Caffe Presto began operations, as well as its profit margin on breakfast

---

[9] The Gilbertian situation is an absurd state of affairs arrived at by logical argument. Darlington, The World of Gilbert and Sullivan 194 (1950). Consider, for example, the resolution in Gilbert and Sullivan's Ruddigore. The protagonist, Sir Ruthven Murgatroyd, under an ancient witch's curse that afflicts his line, must commit one crime each day or die. An honest man, he desires desperately to escape that burden. The following dialog occurs:
Ruthven: — "an idea has just occurred to me. A Baronet of Ruddigore can only die through refusing to commit his daily crime."
Roderick (an ancestor who is dead): "No doubt."
Ruthven: "Therefore, to refuse to commit a daily crime is tantamount to suicide!"
Roderick: "It would seem so."
Ruthven: "But suicide is, itself, a crime — and so, by your own showing, you ought never to have died at all!"
Roderick: "I see — I understand! Then I'm practically alive!"
Ruthven: "Undoubtedly!"

items. From that evidence the jury could calculate to a reasonable degree of certainty the profits the tenant would have expected to enjoy during the remaining years of its lease, had Caffe Presto not been operating. See *Parker* v. *Levin*, 285 Mass. 125, 128 (1934); *Kabatchnick* v. *Hanover-Elm Bldg. Corp.*, 331 Mass. 366, 372 (1954).

4. Measure of the landlord's recovery of rent due. a. Before termination of the lease. By the time the summary process component of this litigation came for trial, the tenant had vacated the premises, and the issue was the tenant's liability to the landlord for rent (see note 5, *supra*). The judge found rent due in the aggregate of $50,957.81. Under the lease, the tenant was also liable for legal fees and costs attendant on the rent collection action. Those fees and costs the judge found to be $3,678.75. Both sides have appealed from the summary process judgment.[10]

For its part, the tenant claims that, rather than assessing to the tenant — until the termination of the lease — the monthly rent established under the lease, the judge should have obliged the tenant to pay rent as diminished by the consequences of the landlord's failure to enforce the noncompetition clause. As we understand the tenant's position, the judge should have made a finding as to the fair market value per year of the noncompetition provision and should then have deducted that amount from the annual lease rent.

The judge was right not to do so for two reasons. First, the judge had already assessed damages against the landlord for breach of the noncompetition clause; to have set the consequences of the breach against the rent would have granted tenant double recovery for the same wrong. Second, a provision in the lease, par. 7 of the rider, had provided that "Tenant shall not be entitled in any case to off-set against its liability for rent any sum owed to Tenant by Landlord." Although the traditional rule of independent covenants has been subject to question and some attrition, it still adheres when the parties to the governing lease have so stated. *Holmes Realty Trust* v. *Granite City Storage Co.*, 25 Mass. App. Ct. 272, 277-278 & n.2 (1988). See also Restatement (Second) of Property, Landlord & Tenant s. 7.1 (1977); Bloom et al., Lease Drafting

---

[10] We shall discuss later in this opinion why we think the tenant's notice of appeal from the summary judgment was timely filed, a point the landlord has put in question.

in Massachusetts s.s. 6.84-6.87 (MCLE 1996). The lease in this case was the product of tough negotiation by experienced parties and their counsel. Particularly in such circumstances, courts should not "undertake to be wiser than the parties." *Guerin* v. *Stacy*, 175 Mass. 595, 597 (1900).

b. After termination of the lease. By written notice, the landlord terminated the lease, effective September 6, 1994, for nonpayment of rent. There is no dispute about the date or legal sufficiency of the notice. The tenant did not vacate the premises until some seven weeks later, on October 31, 1994. The judge reasoned that as the lease had been terminated, the tenant had become a tenant at sufferance during the holdover period and that the correct measure for a use and occupancy charge was the then current fair rental value of the premises. In the absence of a provision in the lease requiring lease payments beyond the lease term, that is the correct measure of damages. *Ghoti Estates, Inc.* v. *Freda's Capri Restaurant, Inc.*, 332 Mass. 17, 26-27 (1954). See *Swift* v. *Boyd*, 202 Mass. 26, 28 (1909); *Lowell Hous. Authy.* v. *Save-Mor Furniture Stores, Inc.*, 346 Mass. 426, 431 (1963); G. L. c. 186, s. 3.

Since October 28, 1987, the date of the lease, the real estate market in Boston had suffered a severe sinking spell. By the time of the holdover period, the base lease rent was $4,523 per month. There was evidence to support the judge's finding that the fair market rent for the space had for the September to October, 1994, period slipped to $1,774 per month. Based on that figure, the judge assessed against the tenant a charge of $3,206.50 for the entire holdover period.

The landlord argues that there was a provision in the lease for the payment of rent beyond the lease term and that it was entitled to the lease rent for the period, which came to $11,375.10, an amount that was $8,168.60 greater than the judge had allowed for use and occupancy. Section 19.B of the lease, which deals with the subject of default by the tenant is, however, a study in opacity. In pertinent part it provides:

"[I]f the Tenant shall fail to pay the base rent ... at the option of the Landlord, the Tenant's right of possession shall thereupon cease and terminate and the Landlord shall be entitled to the possession of the Premises by process of law, any notice to quit, or of intention to re-enter the same being hereby expressly waived by Tenant.... In the event of such re-entry by process of law or otherwise the Tenant nevertheless agrees to remain liable for any and all damage, deficiency or loss of rent which the Landlord may sustain, whether or not the Landlord re-lets the Premises; and in the event of such re-entry Landlord may accelerate the rent for the balance of the term...."

Looking at this language, the trial judge came to the conclusion, we think correctly, that it distinguished between a notice of termination and a notice of entry or an act of entry. Liability for rent, under the lease as written, accrued only if the landlord elected the entry option. Although a lessor may for a breach serve notice of entry and thereby work a termination of a lease, *Markey* v. *Smith*, 301 Mass. 64, 73-74 (1938), the reverse does not work. A statement by a lessor in a notice to the tenant that it had terminated the lease, with the demand that the tenant vacate and deliver up the premises does not have the effect of an entry for breach of covenant. *Haymarket Realty Co.* v. *Sullivan*, 249 Mass. 262, 265 (1924). Stavisky & Perkins, Landlord & Tenant Law s. 812 (2d ed. 1993). As the lease text peculiarly limited the tenant's liability for lease rent to cases of entry, the judge properly fell back to the common law standard of a fair market use and occupancy charge for the tenancy at sufferance during the holdover period.[11]

5. *Abuse of process instruction.* The landlord filed a counterclaim to the tenant's complaint of abuse of process, alleging that the complaint of competition from Caffe Presto was a pretext, and that the tenant's ulterior purpose was to extort a reduction in rent. The jury found for the tenant. The landlord claims error in a refusal by the trial judge to give the following requested instruction: "[Landlord] need not win the action brought against it by [tenant] in order to recover for abuse of process." That is a correct statement of law. See *Kelley* v. *Stop & Shop Cos.*, 26 Mass. App. Ct. 557, 558 (1988); Restatement (Second) of Torts s. 682 comment a (1977). Every possible correct statement of law need not, however, be included in jury instructions if the instructions as given are correct and touch on the fundamental elements of the claim. *Corsetti* v. *Stone Co.*, 396

---

[11] No great mystery attends the drafting of a provision that holds a defaulting and holdover tenant to the lease rent. For example: "In the event that this Lease is terminated as the result of an Event of Default by Tenant, Tenant covenants (a) to pay punctually to Landlord all the sums which Tenant covenants in this Lease to pay in the same manner and to the same extent and at the same time as if this Lease had not been terminated ...." Bloom et al., Lease Drafting in

Mass. 1, 14-15 (1985). *General Dynamics Corp.* v. *Federal Pac. Elec. Co.*, 20 Mass. App. Ct. 677, 684 (1985). *Salamone* v. *Riczler*, 32 Mass. App. Ct. 429, 433 (1992). The judge had instructed as follows:

"In order to prove its claim of an abuse of process, [landlord] must first prove that [tenant] used legal process; and second, that [tenant] did so knowingly and wrongfully to accomplish some ulterior purpose; that is, a purpose for which the process was not designed or intended or some illegitimate purpose, and then, of course, damages."

The judge then proceeded to explicate to the jury each of those elements. The instruction was correct based on the authority of cases such as *Datacomm Interface, Inc.* v. *Computerworld, Inc.*, 396 Mass. 760, 775-776 (1986), and *Kelley* v. *Stop & Shop Cos.*, 26 Mass. App. Ct. at 558.

6. Timeliness of the summary process appeal. When we previously considered summary process damages, we bypassed a procedural point, raised by the landlord, that the tenant's appeal was not timely and ought to have been dismissed. The landlord filed its summary process action under G. L. c. 239 in the Boston Municipal Court on September 19, 1994. The tenant moved to consolidate that eviction action with the contract action it had filed with Superior Court on June 22, 1993, and which was scheduled for trial on October 17, 1994. The trial judge in the Superior Court allowed the motion, reserving the summary process action for her decision after trial on the other issues. See G. L. c. 223, s. 2B; *Nautican Realty Co.* v. *Nantucket Shipyard, Inc.*, 28 Mass. App. Ct. 902, 903 (1989). Each case retained its separate docket number. The parties stipulated that, in making her decision on the summary process questions, the judge could consider any evidence admitted in the contract action. Judgments in the consolidated cases were entered on May 11, 1995. The tenant filed its notice of appeal twenty-nine days later on June 9, 1995, within the thirty-day period allowed by Mass. R.A.P. 4, as amended, 395 Mass. 1110 (1985). The rub is that the appeal period from a summary process judgment is ten days. G. L. c. 239, s. 5.

We have required strict adherence to the short period for claiming an appeal prescribed by G. L. c. 239, s. 5. *Liberty Mobilehome Sales, Inc.* v. *Bernard*, 6 Mass. App. Ct. 914 (1978). *Jones* v. *Manns*, 33 Mass. App. Ct. 485, 488-489 (1992). The process provided for in c. 239 is designed, after all, to be summary. See *Hodge* v. *Klug*, 33 Mass. App. Ct. 746, 757 (1992). Once the summary process case was consolidated with the contract case, however, it lost its fast track identity and underwent a metamorphosis into a standard civil action. The facts bearing on the summary process action were developed in the course of the jury trial of the contract claim. The cases had become integrated, and we think it appropriate, in those circumstances, to apply to the various aspects of those cases the same period for filing a notice of appeal — the thirty-day one established by Mass. R.A.P. 4. Orion's notice of appeal was, therefore, timely.

7. *The c. 93A claim.* The trial judge concluded that, although the landlord had committed a breach of the noncompetition provision, it had not acted unfairly or deceptively, and it had not violated G. L. c 93A, s.s. 2 and 11. The landlord did not violate a provision of the lease to gain an economic advantage or to extort a concession. Compare *Anthony's Pier Four, Inc.* v. *HBC Assocs.*, 411 Mass. 451, 474, 476 (1991), with *Atkinson* v. *Rosenthal*, 33 Mass. App. Ct. 219, 226 (1992). There was no evidence that the landlord obtained any specific economic advantage from the Caffe Presto cart which, it will be remembered, operated under a sublease from Brandy Pete's. The landlord and tenant had a genuine difference of opinion about the meaning of the "no other deli" clause. That was not remarkable if one bears in mind that the tenant, in order to make its case, was bound to concede that the noncompetition clause, proposed by its own counsel, was not self-defining. This was an ordinary contract dispute without conduct that was unethical, immoral, oppressive, or unscrupulous. *Levings* v. *Forbes & Wallace, Inc.*, 8 Mass. App. Ct. 498, 504 (1979). Not every unlawful act is automatically an unfair or deceptive one. *Mechanics Natl. Bank* v. *Killeen*, 377 Mass. 100, 109 (1979).

Judgments affirmed.

COMMONWEALTH *v.* KENNETH E. BUZZELL

49 Mass. App. Ct. 902

April 25, 2000

RESCRIPT

Sometimes a dog's bark can be as bad as its bite. Thus, G.L. c. 140, s. 157, as amended by St. 1985, c. 455, authorizes selectmen of a town to determine that a dog "is a nuisance by reason of ... excessive barking" and to "make such order concerning ... the disposal of such dog as may be deemed necessary." The selectmen of Phillipston issued an order on April 5, 1993, directing the defendant Buzzell, a breeder of dogs, to remove his dogs because they barked too much. That order Buzzell challenged in District Court, as was his right under s. 157, but without success. Three years later, in 1996, dogs were still on Buzzell's premises — and barking. Failure to comply with a removal order is a criminal offense under the last sentence of the first paragraph of s. 157. Under that provision, the Commonwealth brought proceedings against Buzzell charging him with sixteen violations of the dog removal order. The Commonwealth's complaint was tried in District Court to a jury of six, which returned verdicts of guilty on all sixteen counts. The trial judge imposed sixteen thirty-day sentences in a house of correction, to be served consecutively.

1. *Required finding of not guilty.* Buzzell's principal claim of error is that he was entitled to a required finding of not guilty — for which he timely moved — because the Commonwealth had failed to prove that at least one of the dogs present on the defendant's property on the date of the removal order, April 5, 1993, was still present and barking during the period, March, 1996, through September, 1996, that the sixteen counts in the complaint encompass. One might have thought that point disposed of in *Commonwealth* v. *Ferreri*, 30 Mass. App. Ct. 966 (1991), a similar case, in which we wrote, "It was not incumbent upon the Commonwealth to show that the dogs in the defendant's possession on

the dates of the complaints were identical in being and number to the dogs which were the subject of the removal order." *Id.* at 968. The answer to the defendant's "at least one identical dog" argument is that G.L. c. 140, s. 157, as explicated in the *Ferreri* case, recognizes the fungibility of barking dogs. The mischief to be corrected is excessive barking and whether the source of the barking on the premises is Fang or Fido is not of the essence. Had the defendant kept a quiet dog on his premises after the removal order, the case might stand differently.

2. Multiple convictions. On appeal, the Commonwealth correctly concedes that Buzzell failed to comply with only one order, and that it was error to convict him of sixteen offenses. Violation over a period of time of a nuisance statute such as G.L. c. 140, S.157, constitutes a continuing offense, not multiple offenses. *Wells* v. *Commonwealth*, 12 Gray 326 , 328-329 (1859). Cf. *Carpenter v. Texaco, Inc.* 419 Mass. 581 , 583 n.4 (1995). When the Legislature intends that each day that a violation continues shall count as a separate offense, it expressly so provides. See, e.g., G.L. c. 131, s. 40, par. 32.

3. Conclusion. We affirm the conviction on the first count charged under G.L. c. 140, s. 157, and remand to the District Court for (1) dismissal of the remaining fifteen counts of the complaint against the defendant; and (2) vacating of all but one of the thirty-day sentences.

So ordered.

Matthew S. Robinowitz for the defendant.
Susanne Levsen, Assistant District Attorney, for the Commonwealth.

Editor's note: A short, unsigned opinion of the Court is called a rescript opinion. A rescript opinion may be unsigned, but it is not necessarily anonymous. Chief Justice Mark Green said about this opinion, "Rudy's style was such that his hand was obvious even in a brief rescript opinion, issued without authoring attribution. When I opened the daily advance sheets on the morning of April 25, 2000 and saw the opening line of Commonwealth v. Buzzell, 49 Mass. App. Ct. 902 (2000), I knew immediately who had written it."

Regina Alfonso *v.* Edward Lowney

11 Mass. App. Ct. 338

Bristol. December 4, 1980 – February 12, 1981.

Present: HALE, C.J., CUTTER, & KASS, JJ.

CIVIL ACTION commenced in the Superior Court on February 11, 1976.

The case was tried before *Mitchell*, J.

Philip N. Beauregard, City Solicitor, for the defendant.

Scott Edward Charnas for the plaintiff.

KASS, J.

A wolf in the New Bedford Buttonwood Park Zoo, a city facility, pushed enough of his snout through his pen to bite the plaintiff's finger. This action against the superintendent of parks of New Bedford alleged negligence in permitting the existence of a pen from which a wolf, doing what carnivores will, could bite someone on the viewing side of the enclosure. There was a verdict for the plaintiff. From the judgment on the verdict, the defendant has appealed.

1. The incident occurred in 1975. Accordingly, this case is governed by *Vaughan* v. *Commonwealth*, 377 Mass. 914 (1979), which held that settled common law principles concerning governmental immunity and exceptions to it would apply to claims against governmental bodies and their employees as to causes of action arising before August 16, 1977. On and after that date, events giving rise to a tort claim against the Commonwealth and its subdivisions (including municipalities) became controlled as to substance and procedure by G.L. c. 258, as appearing in St. 1978, c. 512, § 15. As to effective dates, see St. 1978, c. 512, § 16. See *Lemasurier* v. *Pepperell*, 10 Mass. App. Ct. 96, 98 (1980).

Although *Whitney* v. *Worcester*, 373 Mass. 208 (1977), expressed an intent, if the Legislature did not act, to abandon the misfeasance-nonfeasance distinction in suits against a public officer, the fact of subsequent legislative action gave continued life to the traditional principles regarding the immunity of a public officer which are restated at page 220 of the Whitney decision. Under the old rule, "[P]ublic officers engaged wholly in the performance of public duties are liable only for their own acts of misfeasance in connection with ministerial matters." *Id.* at 220, quoting from *Fulgoni* v. *Johnston*, 302 Mass. 421, 423 (1939). Nonfeasance, the omission of an act which a person ought to do, creates no liability. Misfeasance is the improper doing of an act. *Trum* v. *Paxton*, 329 Mass. 434, 438 (1952). *Whitney* v. *Worcester*, 373 Mass. at 220. Compare the provisions which now appear in G.L. c. 258, § 10.

There was no evidence that the defendant had any direct role in the design, construction or maintenance of the wolf pen. He is not personally liable for mistakes which subordinates might have made. *Trum* v. *Paxton*, 329 Mass. at 438. Therefore, the motion for judgment notwithstanding the verdict should have been allowed. See *O'Shaughnessy* v. *Besse*, 7 Mass. App. Ct. 727, 728 (1979).

2. Although, on the view we take of the case, we need not reach the point, we note that the judge did not charge the jury on the misfeasance-nonfeasance distinction. The defendant's counsel called this defect in the charge to the judge's attention after the conclusion of the instructions to the jury.[1] The judge erred in refusing to amend his charge because the defendant had made no request for such an instruction prior to commencement of the charge. Although it is a good practice for a litigant to request certain instructions before the charge, it is not legally necessary to do so. Parties are entitled to an accurate statement of the law for the guidance of the jury. *Hughes* v. *Whiting*, 276 Mass. 76, 79 (1931). Smith Zobel, Rules Practice § 51.3 (1977). Compare *Narkin* v. *Springfield*, 5 Mass. App. Ct. 489, 491-492 (1977). Parenthetically, we observe that the judge's charge also did not mention contributory negligence, of which the evidence was redolent. We also note that upon concluding his charge the judge left the courtroom without affording

---

[1] Hedging his bets on whether *Whitney* announced a change in the law or just an intent to change the law, counsel also asked for — and was denied — an instruction on the ministerial-nonministerial duty distinction. See *Whitney* v. *Worcester*, 373 Mass. at 220-221. Compare G.L. c. 258, § 10.

counsel a chance to object to the charge. This conduct effectively nullified the right afforded counsel by Mass.R.Civ.P. 51(b), 365 Mass. 816 (1974), to object to instructions before the jury retires. The record reflects that defense counsel instantly took steps (counsel were ushered into the judge's lobby within five minutes of the recess) to see the judge in his lobby for the purpose of making known the defendant's objections.

Judgment is reversed and a new judgment shall be entered for the defendant.

So ordered.

CLARISSA ALLEN *v.* ROSS F. BATCHELDER, trustee, & others[1]

17 Mass. App. Ct. 453

Dukes County. November 14, 1983 – January 27, 1984.

Present: PERRETTA, KASS, & WARNER, JJ.

PETITION filed in the Land Court Department on July 27, 1978.
The case was heard by *Randall, J.*
John H. Wyman for Ross F. Batchelder.
Jane Maslow Cohen for the plaintiff.

KASS, J.

Sebastian, the tobacco-chewing sheep, would have been disconcerted by this appeal. His status as a Martha's Vineyard tourist attraction was a function of his visibility on the Allen farm, astride the South Road in Chilmark.

Sebastian could not have achieved the modest notoriety he enjoyed without tenure of the Allen farm by his owners, Henry and Maude Allen. The appellant, Batchelder, has called in question the exclusivity of the Allens' title, which has come down to Clarissa Allen (Clarissa). Batchelder espouses a theory that his predecessors in title, nonpossessory cotenants, were not affirmatively ousted from possession of the locus and that, therefore, the Allen family could not, as the Land Court judge determined, have acquired exclusive title to the farm by adverse possession. In light of 150 years of well developed case

---

[1] Three other answers were filed by persons who expressed an interest in Clarissa Allen's registration petition. They either settled or were otherwise satisfied with the Land Court's judgment. Batchelder is the only appellant.

law, we conclude that the appellant's position is so untenable as to be frivolous.

The case began with a petition in the Land Court under G. L. c. 185, Section 1, for registration.[2] Clarissa occupies the locus, consisting of 116.7 acres, which her forebears acquired between 1762 and 1857. Land Court examiners (there were two) reported a record defect in Clarissa's title which developed upon the death of Tristam Allen, II, in 1864.[3] Tristam left undivided fractional interests in a portion of the Allen farm to his widow, Tamson. Neither she, nor persons to whom her interests passed by devise, who were outside the Allen family, ever occupied the farm or made claim to any rents and profits from it. Batchelder claims under that line of title. Clarissa's line, in contrast, lived on and worked the farm actively.

After a long trial, the Land Court judge found that, at least from 1892, "the Allen farm was possessed by various members of the Allen family to the exclusion of any cotenant in common." Clarissa's grandfather, Henry Allen, was well known in Chilmark. He held office as selectman, assessor, overseer of the poor and town moderator, manifesting a bent for public life which a witness, Captain Poole, attributed to Henry's being "lazier than hell ... he was a typical small-town politician. He'd pat you on the back wherever you met him and agree with you 100 percent." Manifestly, his occupancy of the Allen farm was widely known and far from concealed. Maude, his wife, was the sheep's patroness. Henry's son, Roger, industrious by any measure, ran the farm and used some of the farm's outbuildings for a contracting business. Roger died in 1967, and farming came to a halt. His widow, however, continued to pay taxes on the locus, aggressively posted no trespassing signs, and routinely checked the farm. Clarissa, in 1975, came to live on the farm and to rejuvenate it.

That the Allen family possessed the locus actually, openly and notoriously for at least ninety years is not in controversy. As the judge observed in his detailed and careful decision, the evidence on this score

---

[2] Catherine B. Allen, Clarissa Allen's mother, joined in the complaint seeking registration. Subsequently, she conveyed her interest to Clarissa.

[3] Record title was good in the case of one of the eight parcels included in the locus.

was overwhelming.[4] Sebastian, the sheep, was but a minor example of how closely the Allen family were identified with the farm by residents of Martha's Vineyard. The judge found an equally strong case had been made that the Allen's possession was adverse and nonpermissive and that, accordingly, they had acquired good title by adverse possession to the seven parcels tainted with a record defect. For the elements of adverse possession, see *Ryan* v. *Stavros*, 348 Mass. 251, 262 (1964).

Batchelder's attack is on whether the Allens' possession was adverse and nonpermissive. It is uncontroverted that Clarissa's line was never aware of the claim now pressed on behalf of the Batchelder line and that no one in the Batchelder line was ever cognizant of the potential for that claim until publication of the registration petition in 1980 was called to Batchelder's attention by a William J. Devine. The judge found expressly that during the ninety-year period upon which he concentrated, no claim of title by Batchelder's predecessors was ever made.

Batchelder supports his claim with the argument that the interest of a cotenant cannot be wiped out by prescription without an ouster and, more to the point, communication of that ouster to the absent cotenant. It is correct that sole possession by one tenant in common is not in itself adverse to the interest of a nonpossessory cotenant; it could be consistent with the right of the cotenant. *Rickard* v. *Rickard*, 13 Pick. 251, 253-254 (1832). As early as that 1832 case, however, it was regarded by Chief Justice Shaw as equally "well settled, that a long exclusive and uninterrupted possession by one, without any possession, or claim for profits by the other, is evidence from which a jury may and ought to infer an actual ouster." Ibid. There need be no "turning out by the shoulders" to manifest a decisive intent to occupy to the exclusion of the absent cotenant. *Doe* v. *Prosser*, 1 Cowp. 217, 218, 98 Eng. Rep. 1052 (1774).[5] The principle has been many times restated or applied. *Lefavour* v. *Homan*, 3 Allen 354, 355 (1862). *Ingalls* v. *Newhall*, 139 Mass. 268, 273

---

[4] The extensive evidence was adduced by Clarissa. Batchelder offered none.

[5] *Doe* v. *Prosser* was the case which had caused the question to be "well settled" so far as Chief Justice Shaw was concerned. Lord Mansfield in that case expressed himself as "clearly of opinion ... that an undisturbed and quiet possession for such a length of time [forty years] is a sufficient ground for the jury to presume an actual ouster ..." *Doe* v. *Prosser*, 1 Cowp. at 219, 98 Eng. Rep. at 1053. Justice Aston in his opinion in the same case was moved to ask: "What is adverse possession or ouster, if the uninterrupted receipt of the rents and profits without account for near 40 years is not?" *Ibid.*

(1885). *Joyce* v. *Dyer*, 189 Mass. 64, 67-68 (1905). Nickerson v. Nickerson, 235 Mass. 348, 352-353 (1920). *Snow* v. *E.L. Dauphinais*, Inc., 13 Mass. App. Ct. 330, 334 (1982). In those cases the periods of exclusive possession which worked an ouster varied from thirty to forty-seven years. Clarissa's line has possessed the Allen farm for not less than ninety years. "[M]en do not ordinarily sleep on their rights for so long a period, and a strong presumption arises that actual proof of the original ouster has become lost by lapse of time." *Lefavour* v. *Homan, supra* at 355-356.

It distorts the cases cited to find in them a requirement that the absent cotenant must have knowledge that he is dispossessed. Knowledge, when the absent cotenant appeared to have it, was a convenient factor in the equation in *Ingalls* v. *Newhall, supra* at 273-274, and in *Nickerson* v. *Nickerson, supra* at 353. The underlying inquiry, however, has always been what knowledge the absent party "must be deemed to have had." *Ingalls* v. *Newhall, supra* at 274. Precisely how long a possession should be to raise a presumption of ouster depends on many circumstances, ibid., but it is apparent from the cases that ninety years is far more than enough. *Lefavour* v. *Homan, supra* at 355, emphasizes that absence and failure to make a claim, "if unexplained or controlled by any evidence tending to show a reason for such neglect or omission to assert a right," furnishes evidence from which the trier of fact ought to infer an actual ouster and adverse possession. Requiring actual knowledge of disseisin "would deprive the principle of prescription of much of its value in quieting controversy and giving sanction to long continued usages." *Foot* v. *Bauman*, 333 Mass. 214, 217-218 (1955). Long dormant claims to title could rise from the dust bin of history and many titles would become unsettled. This is particularly so in a case such as the instant one, where the absent parties did not live near the locus. Ada Cleveland, who took from Tamson, and her chain of title down to Batchelder, all lived off island. See also *Ottavia* v. *Savarese*, 338 Mass. 330, 333-334 (1959), which disposes of the proposition that the Allens' possession needed to be consciously adverse to the Batchelder line, i.e., that the Allens needed to be aware of the Batchelder claim to defeat it.

We have dwelled at some length on the extensive and decisive case law which defeats this appeal because it bears on how we deal with a motion by the appellee, Clarissa Allen, for damages and costs under

Mass.R.A.P. 25, and Mass.R.A.P. 26, both as amended, 378 Mass. 925 (1979). Rule 25 authorizes assessment of damages, as well as double costs of the appeal, in instances where the appeal is frivolous. *Mills* v. *Carlow*, 15 Mass. App. Ct. 1104 (1983). See *Good Hope Refineries, Inc.* v. *Brashear*, 588 F.2d 846, 848 (1st Cir. 1978). See the cases collected in 9 Moore's Federal Practice par. 238.02 (2d ed. 1983), in which the cognate Federal rule (Fed.R.A.P. 38) has been applied. See also *Katz* v. *Savitsky*, 10 Mass. App. Ct. 792, 798 n.8 (1980). When the law is well settled, when there can be no reasonable expectation of a reversal, an appeal is frivolous. See Note, Penalties for Frivolous Appeals, 43 Harv. L.Rev. 113, 114-116 (1929).

An appeal should not, however, be tarred as frivolous because it presents an argument that is novel, unusual or ingenious, or urges adoption of a new principle of law or revision of an old one. Compare G. L. c. 231, Section 6F. In the instant case the appeal covers no ground not gone over by the cases, and the appellant has urged no policy consideration which would warrant reappraisal of the settled rule. Indeed, leading authorities are consistent with the Massachusetts decisions. Restatement of Property Section 458 comment i, illustration 9 (1944). 2 & 3 American Law of Property Sections 8.56 & 15.3 (1952). 7 Powell, The Law of Real Property par. 1013[2] (Rohan rev. ed. 1982).

Here, the appellant's case had lost all vestige of merit after the Land Court judge made his decision. A Land Court judge's findings in registration proceedings carry weight even beyond that generally accorded by an appellate court to findings of a trial judge. *Norton* v. *West*, 8 Mass. App. Ct. 348, 350 (1979). Coupled with the strong evidence built up in favor of Clarissa, there was no hope for the appellant on any issue of fact and, indeed, the appellant, Batchelder, attempted no argument aimed at the judge's findings.

The judge's decision also contained a discussion of the relevant authorities, all of which had been copiously cited and discussed in a posttrial memorandum filed on behalf of Clarissa. Before he launched his appeal, therefore, the appellant was fully aware of the powerful precedents built up over the years against the appellant's position. There was no reasonable expectation of a reversal; the appeal was frivolous.

Another aspect of the case warrants comment. Batchelder, a candid witness, testified he resided in Winthrop and knew nothing about the

Allen farm on Martha's Vineyard or a potential claim to an interest in it until, as we noted above, William J. Devine brought the possibility to attention. Devine proposed that he would pay the costs of mounting a legal campaign to assert the Batchelder claim and that he (Devine) and Batchelder would share the net proceeds of anything they realized from the litigation. To that end, Batchelder conveyed his interest in the locus, whatever it might be, to a trust of which he and Devine were equal beneficiaries.

This is the third occasion within a year in which we have come across the same pattern of a title challenge induced and financed by Devine. See *Devine* v. *Nantucket*, 16 Mass. App. Ct. 548 (1983), and *Hilde* v. *Dixon*, 16 Mass. App. Ct. 981 (1983). He appears to be a bounty hunter in troubled titles. The appellee has not raised the issue of champerty, but it is a subject to which a court may turn its attention on its own initiative. See *Sherwin-Williams Co.* v. *J. Mannos & Sons*, 287 Mass. 304, 312 (1934); *Baskin* v. *Pass*, 302 Mass. 338, 342 (1939). Champerty is the maintenance, at the champertor's expense, of a legal action in consideration of profit out of the action, if any. *Sherwin-Williams Co.* v. *J. Mannos & Sons*, 287 Mass. at 312. *Pupecki* v. *James Madison Corp.*, 376 Mass. 212, 219 (1978). Devine is not a lawyer, but it is not necessary to be a member of the bar to make a champertous agreement. *Graustein* v. *Boston & Maine R.R.*, 304 Mass. 23, 27 (1939). *Gill* v. *Richmond Co-op. Assn.*, 309 Mass. 73, 76 (1941).

Champerty does not presuppose that the case to be maintained is a frivolous one. It is the latter characteristic which provides the occasion for invocation of Mass.R.A.P. 25. This case's champertous antecedents, however, bear on our willingness to apply the sanctions available under the rule and, as well, color our view of the damages which are appropriate.

Accordingly, the appellee, Clarissa Allen, is to have $5,000 damages on account of her legal fees for the appeal[6], as well as double costs of the appeal.

---

[6] In support of the appellee's motion for damages and costs, which was filed before oral argument and discussed at argument, her lawyer filed an affidavit of the estimated time spent in preparation and presentation of the appellee's brief and argument (slightly in excess of forty hours) and her (the lawyer's) hourly charge. We consider the time and hourly charge reasonable. See generally *First Natl. Bank* v. *Brink*, 372 Mass. 257, 265-266 (1977); *Salem Realty Co. v. Matera*, 10 Mass. App. Ct. 571, 576-577 (1980).

The judgment is affirmed. Damages and costs shall be assessed in the Land Court as above provided.

So ordered.

RICHARD A. GOREN & OTHERS[1] V. ROYAL INVESTMENTS INCORPORATED & OTHERS[2]

25 Mass. App. Ct. 137

Suffolk. October 20, 1987 – December 9, 1987.

Present: DREBEN, KASS, & FINE, JJ.

CIVIL ACTION commenced in the Superior Court Department on July 18, 1984.

The case was heard by *David H. Kopelman*, J., sitting under statutory authority.

Anthony E. Battelle (*Robert M. Ruzzo* with him) for Paramount Associates.

Regina L. Quinlan for Royal Investments Incorporated.

Robert B. Carpenter (*Joseph S. Ayoub, Jr.*, with him) for Richard A. Goren & others.

KASS, J.

Once again we consider in what circumstances a writing, which by context or by terms contemplates a more formal agreement, may nonetheless serve as a binding contract.

We summarize the facts which present the problem. After a course of negotiations during May, 1984, Piatt Associates and Richard A. Goren (collectively called "Opera") as buyer, and Royal Investments Incorporated ("Royal"), as seller, signed a document as of June 6, 1984, contemplating the sale by Royal to Opera of the premises at 565-567 Washington Street, Boston (the "locus"). That document bore the caption "Offer to Purchase." Over the signature of Opera were the words "SUBMITTED BY" and over the signature of Royal there appeared the words "ACCEPTED BY." Prior to the signed document of

---

[1] James Piatt and Thomas Piatt. With Goren, the Piatts formed a general partnership called Opera Development Associates.

[2] F.D. Rich Co., Inc., and Joseph J. Berlandi, who are partners with Royal Investments Incorporated in a partnership known as Paramount Associates.

June 6, 1984, there had been four drafts which successively offered improved terms to the seller but which were not acceptable to it.

The fifth, and accepted, draft, i.e., that of June 6, 1984, offered a price of $762,000, entirely in cash. There were provisions which provided for: sequential deposits (aggregating $50,000); the handling of then current leases and the making of new ones; a closing date; and payment of a broker's commission by the seller. Under a caption which read, "PURCHASE AND SALE," there appeared the following sentence: "A mutually acceptable Purchase and Sale Agreement shall be executed within four weeks of acceptance of this offer."

Before a purchase and sale agreement was signed, Royal received an offer to buy its property that was $78,000 higher than that which Opera had made. Royal became inattentive to calls from Opera or the broker. Although it had expected Royal, as seller, to proffer a purchase and sale agreement, Opera had an agreement prepared (on the 1978 edition of the Greater Boston Real Estate Board form), which incorporated the terms of the June 6th document. Opera then tendered signed copies of that agreement to Royal. On July 11, 1984, twenty-four hours after it had signed an agreement to sell to the party that had offered the better price, Royal informed Opera that their deal was off. "[W]e cannot sign this agreement," Royal explained, "in that we cannot guarantee the removal of the Moto-Photo tenant from the building." Two days earlier on July 9th, Royal had, for a price, in fact secured the agreement of Moto-Photo to vacate its space in the locus.

Among his detailed findings the trial judge found as follows: The document dated June 6, 1984, and countersigned by the seller on June 7, 1984, had been the end product of active negotiations. It constituted more than a preliminary expression of intent or draft for discussion purposes. Rather, the parties intended to be bound as of June 7, 1984, by the provisions of the June 6th document, and execution of a purchase and sale agreement was no more than a formality intended to tidy up ministerial and nonessential terms of the bargain. The transaction was not particularly complex and did not require intricate final documents. Assertions by Melone, Royal's principal officer, that he would not have agreed to boilerplate provisions in the agreement tendered by Opera (relating, e.g., to state of the title, insurance, liquidated damages in the event of buyer's default) were not credible because the same provisions appeared in the agreement Royal signed to get the higher price.

The provision in the June 6th document looking to execution of a purchase and sale agreement, the judge concluded, contemplated that the parties would exercise good faith in attempting to draft and negotiate such an agreement. Royal, the judge found, did not act in good faith. In its refusal to execute the agreement tendered by Opera, it "was motivated entirely by the increased financial benefits which Royal would realize if it were able to convey the property to Paramount Associates at a purchase price of $840,000 ...." Judgment entered requiring Royal to convey the locus to Opera for $762,000, the price in the June 6th document.

We are, of course, bound by the judge's findings of facts unless they are clearly erroneous. Mass.R.Civ.P. 52(a), 365 Mass. 816 (1974). *First Pennsylvania Mortgage Trust* v. *Dorchester Sav. Bank*, 395 Mass. 614, 621-622 (1985). *Connecticut Jr. Republic* v. *Doherty*, 20 Mass. App. Ct. 107, 110 (1985). On appeal Royal prudently does not dissipate its energy in rebutting the implicit finding of the judge that it suffered a spell of moral abandon. Rather, relying on *Rosenfield* v. *United States Trust Co.*, 290 Mass. 210 (1935), and its progeny[3], Royal urges that the judge was clearly in error in finding that the parties had agreed on all significant points. The clause contemplating execution of a purchase and sale agreement, Royal contends, was a talisman of the inchoate quality of the June 6th document.

To be sure, as the court observed in the Rosenfield case, language looking to execution of a final written agreement justifies a strong inference that significant items on the agenda of the transaction are still open and, hence, that the parties do not intend to be bound. *Id.* at 216. See also *Doten* v. *Chase*, 237 Mass. 218, 220 (1921); *Chapin* v. *Ruby*, 321 Mass. 512, 515 (1947); *Currier v. Kosinski*, 24 Mass. App. Ct. 106, 108 (1987). Cf. *Capezzuto* v. *John Hancock Mut. Life Ins. Co.*, 394 Mass. 399, 403 (1985). If, however, the parties have agreed upon all material terms, it may be inferred that the purpose of a final document which the parties

---

[3] *Saxon Theatre Corp.* v. *Sage*, 347 Mass. 662, 666-667 (1964). *Mann* v. *Wolff*, 352 Mass. 776 (1967). *Blair* v. *Cifrino*, 355 Mass. 706, 709-710 (1969). *Lucey* v. *Hero Intl. Corp.*, 361 Mass. 569, 574-575 (1972). *Mendel Kern, Inc.* v. *Workshop, Inc.*, 400 Mass. 277, 279 (1987). *Tull* v. *Mister Donut Dev. Corp.*, 7 Mass. App. Ct. 626, 630 (1979). *JRY Corp.* v. *LeRoux*, 18 Mass. App. Ct. 153, 169-172 (1984).

agree to execute is to serve as a polished memorandum of an already binding contract. Ibid. Although the parties exchanged slogans of agreement in the Rosenfield case such as, "that is all settled" and "the deal was closed," it was apparent that the negotiations were imperfect on points which were material and, indeed, weighty in the context of the transaction. *Id.* at 216-217. Rosenfield concerned a jewelry store lease. The parties had not reached agreement on the design and specifications of a store front; the cost of that work and whether the landlord would bear all of it or part of it was unresolved; the parties were dickering over whether the landlord would pay all of the heat or whether the tenant would pay for heat if gross sales (and, consequently rent) did not attain certain minima; and the parties were still debating who would pay for water. *Id.* at 217. In the circumstances, the court saw the parties' preliminary written memorandum of several business points agreed upon as an agreement to reach an agreement, which imposed no obligation on them. *Id.* at 217.

Here, by contrast, all significant economic issues were resolved in the preliminary agreement. The additional matters with which the form purchase and sale agreement treated were subjects such as state of the title, conformance with local law, condition of the premises, extension provision to allow seller time to remove title defects, buyer's right of election to accept a deficient title, performance to be merged in delivery of the deed, use of purchase money to clear title, maintenance of insurance at not less than eighty percent of sound insurable value, assignment of insurance, closing adjustments, holding of deposit by broker, and disclaimer of implied warranties. These points are not without importance and may, on occasion, be the subjects of bargaining. They are, however, subsidiary matters and norms exist for their customary resolution. The form of agreement tendered by Opera conformed to those norms, and the seller does not suggest that at the time of the preliminary agreement there were differences of position on any of the subsidiary points. Compare *Blomendale* v. *Imbrescia, post* 144 (1987).

Royal argues that the highly material matter of delivering the premises free of the tenancy of In and Out Photo of New England, Inc. (known as Moto-Photo), was not resolved. It may not have been resolved between Royal and Moto-Photo (the latter, after the preliminary agreement, appears to have jacked up the price of being bought out), but it was surely resolved in the preliminary agreement, which provided: "Current leases must be terminated by the seller and premises now occupied by Moto-Photo will be delivered vacant at or prior to the closing date."

On the basis of the judge's findings, for which there is support in the record, that the preliminary agreement covered all material points and that the parties so regarded it, the case falls into that category where execution of a more formal instrument "was hardly more than a formality." *Coan* v. *Holbrook*, 327 Mass. 221, 224 (1951).[4] The *Coan* case has both antecedents and progeny. See *Nigro* v. *Conti*, 319 Mass. 480, 482-483 (1946); *Sands* v. *Arruda*, 359 Mass. 591, 596 (1971); *Bridge Enterprises, Inc.* v. *Futurity Thread Co.*, 2 Mass. App. Ct. 243, 248 (1974); *David J. Tierney, Jr., Inc.* v. *Wellington Carpets, Inc.*, 8 Mass. App. Ct. 237, 241 (1979); *Roddy & McNulty Ins. Agency, Inc.* v. *A.A. Proctor & Co.*, 16 Mass. App. Ct. 525, 531-532 (1983); *Cataldo* v. *Zuckerman*, 20 Mass. App. Ct. 731, 737 (1985); *Rand-Whitney Packaging Corp.* v. *Robertson Group, Inc.*, 651 F.Supp. 520, 535-537 (D. Mass. 1986). See Restatement (Second) of Contracts Section 27 (1979).

This is not to say that parties to a preliminary agreement may not provide that they do not intend to be bound until the transaction is buttoned up by a more detailed and formal agreement. There is commercial utility to allowing persons to hug before they marry. See *Tull* v. *Mister Donut Dev. Corp.*, 7 Mass. App. Ct. 626, 631-632 (1979).[5] If "[p]arties to what would otherwise be a bargain and a contract … agree

---

[4] In Coan the preliminary writing provided that the seller would "sign your usual purchase and sale agreement." The words "your usual" are more suggestive of a routine formality than the words "mutually acceptable" which modified "purchase and sale agreement" in the case before us. It is a distinction worth noting but it is not, in our view, dispositive in this case. Forms which contemplate execution of a purchase and sale agreement in a particular form, e.g., the standard purchase and sale agreement published by the local real estate board, are even more suggestive of a routine formality because a promise to execute a particular form comes close to incorporation of a text by reference.

[5] Royal introduced evidence from a real estate broker that it was the custom of the real estate business in Boston to look to a full-blown purchase and sale agreement before regarding parties as bound. The judge was not required to be persuaded and, in any event, custom would not override intent in a particular case, or settled law. See, however, as to the norm, *Currier* v. *Kosinski*, 24 Mass. App. Ct. 106, 108 (1987).

that their legal relations are not to be affected [,] [i]n the absence of any invalidating cause, such a term is respected by the law like any other term ...." Restatement (Second) of Contracts Section 21 comment b (1979). A proviso of that sort should speak plainly, e.g., "The purpose of this document is to memorialize certain business points. The parties mutually acknowledge that their agreement is qualified and that they, therefore, contemplate the drafting and execution of a more detailed agreement. They intend to be bound only by the execution of such an agreement and not by this preliminary document."

So much of the judgment as declared relief is affirmed. Paragraph 3 of the judgment is modified to provide that Royal Investments Incorporated, its agents, employees or attorneys, as owner and seller, shall in or within thirty days of the issuance of the rescript from the Appeals Court deliver to the plaintiffs or their nominee, good and marketable title by quitclaim deed to the premises at 565-567 Washington Street, Boston, in exchange for payment of $762,000 in cash, certified check, cashier's check, or any combination of the three. The balance of the judgment is affirmed.

So ordered.

Exit 1 Properties Limited Partnership *v.* Mobil Oil Corporation

44 Mass. App. Ct. 571

Worcester. January 29, 1998 – April 9, 1998.

Present: KASS, SMITH, & FLANNERY, JJ.

CIVIL ACTION commenced in the Superior Court Department on August 23, 1995.

Case heard by *Herbert F. Travers, Jr.,* J.

Kurt L. Binder, Worcester, for defendant.

Robert E. George, Sturbridge, for plaintiff.

KASS, J.

What Atlantic Richfield Oil Company and Howard Johnson Company had in mind in 1971, when Atlantic Richfield imposed a use restriction on its land along State Route 15, was simple enough. Atlantic Richfield would sell gas and Howard Johnson would sell food. We conclude, as did the Superior Court judge, that the land restriction continues to be of substantial benefit, within the meaning of G.L. c. 184, § 30, to the occupant of the Howard Johnson parcel and is enforceable.

We summarize the subsidiary facts found by the trial judge.[1] In 1971, Atlantic Richfield owned a parcel of land on State Highway 15. On February 18 of that year, Atlantic Richfield conveyed a portion of that real estate to Howard Johnson. That same day, Atlantic Richfield also executed (and thereafter recorded) an instrument entitled "Restrictive Covenant" by which Atlantic Richfield imposed on its remaining land, for the benefit of Howard Johnson, its successors and assigns, a

---

[1] Those findings have support in the evidence, and we accept them. Mass.R.Civ.P. 52(a), 365 Mass. 816 (1974).

restriction that, for fifty years, the remaining land— "shall and will not be used or permitted to be used, directly or indirectly, for a restaurant, motel or hotel or for advertising such business or for the sale of food or beverages except packaged candies, crackers and soft drinks dispensed through vending machines usually on display and for sale in service stations may be sold."[2]

Howard Johnson, at the time, was a well known operator of roadside restaurants. Atlantic Richfield imposed a reciprocal restriction upon the parcel that it conveyed to Howard Johnson, that it not be used for the sale of petroleum products.

In 1994, Mobil Oil Corporation (Mobil) became the operating tenant of the gas station parcel, and Exit 1 Properties Limited Partnership (Exit 1) had become the owner of the restaurant parcel. Through an operating subsidiary, Exit 1 was running two franchise restaurants, a "Roy Rogers" and a "Sbarro." Both provided for on-the-premises eating (dining might be an inflated term). Roy Rogers featured a hamburgers, chicken, roast beef, and french fries menu and Sbarro a pizza and pasta menu.

Until 1987, the gas station (then operated by Atlas Oil Company) confined its nonpetroleum products sales to soda pop, candy, and cigarette vending machines. There were, in 1987, a coffee carafe and "danish" on the counter where customers paid for gas. This occupied a very small space. Some time in 1987, Atlas replaced the drink vending machines with "reach-in" coolers. Otherwise, the product mix and the volume of sales remained approximately the same as before.

Through 1989 and 1990, by a step at a time, the food product line available at the gas station grew and the methods of sale changed. A milk reach-in cooler was installed and then an ice cream chest. Packaged pastries, packaged chips, peanuts, and crackers were displayed on a counter rather than sold through vending machines. Then some packaged sandwiches became available. Next, the gas station management set up a hot dog steamer and provided a microwave oven in which customers could "nuke" items that would benefit from thawing or heating. An executive of Exit 1, Richard Shelton, noticed the accretion of food service at the gas station. Shelton called the principal

---

[2] We have set out the clause exactly as written. We do not endorse its syntax.

of Atlas Oil Company, Irving Singer, to say he could live with a little "overflow" in candy and snacks but not a "flood." Singer said he would respect that limitation. In October, 1991, there were some discussions between Shelton and Singer about operating a "convenience store" at the gas station. Shelton said he could not accept more food business on the gas station site and would insist on compliance with the restrictive covenant. Atlas acquiesced and, indeed, rather than expanding the food line, cut out the hot dogs and sandwiches.

Mobil in 1994 was distinctively expansive. The whole layout in the customer area of the gas station was altered to emphasize food sales. Sandwiches returned as a product line. The beverage coolers grew from two to three and there was a specialty ice cream (Ben & Jerry) chest. A coffee bar offered six or seven "gourmet" coffees from carafes. By 1994, annual food sales were in the range of $170,000 per year compared to $74,000 in 1990. With a profit margin of 35% to 40% on food sales compared to from 10% to 11% on gasoline, the incentive to push food was considerable. It was at this point that Exit 1 made its stand. On August 23, 1995, it filed a complaint to enjoin violation of the restrictive covenant.

1. Application of G.L. c. 184, § 30. Mobil urges that because the trial judge did not, in so many words, find that the restrictive covenant is of substantial benefit to Exit 1, the covenant ought not to be enforced, and that, in any event, the evidence does not support a conclusion that the restriction is of substantial benefit to Exit 1. These contentions are based on so much of G.L. c. 184, § 30, as inserted by St.1961, c. 448, § 1, as provides:

"No restriction shall in any proceeding be enforced or declared to be enforceable ... unless it is determined that the restriction is at the time of the proceeding of actual and substantial benefit to a person claiming rights of enforcement."

In his thorough memorandum of decision, the judge wrote, "the covenant in question was clearly meant to benefit Exit 1 by protecting its restaurant business." Mobil objects that the language quoted falls short of a determination that at the time of trial Exit 1 was, in fact, deriving a substantial benefit from the restriction. But this is surely a cavil. The judge's findings describe the mutual purpose of Atlantic Richfield and Howard Johnson to prevent poaching by either party on the other's line of business. The judge's findings also describe the widening scope of food sales on the automobile service station parcel. It requires no leap of the imagination to understand that to the extent carry-out food more substantial than a candy bar or package of crackers was conveniently available where customers paid for gas, some of those customers would buy something to eat then and there and would be lost as food customers by Roy Rogers and Sbarro. Conversely, customers limited to a choice of peanut crackers and a can of Pepsi-Cola were more likely to opt for the heady delights of the restaurants next door. It is not of consequence that Mobil's offerings were different than those of Roy Rogers and Sbarro; it was food, and offered the customer an eating alternative, i.e., what the use restriction was designed to prevent.

Covenants against competition, such as the restriction we consider in this case, may run with the land and are enforceable if "consistent with a reasonable over-all purpose to develop real estate for commercial use." *Whitinsville Plaza, Inc.* v. *Kotseas,* 378 Mass. 85, 97-98 (1979). In its origins, the restriction was reasonable. Each party invested capital on the strength of an arrangement that it would draw customers travelling on the Boston and New York run, reinforced by the other's business, and not compete with one another. It is no less reasonable twenty years later because the successor of one of the parties finds it tempting to be in both businesses. Purpose, geographic extent, and duration are among criteria for testing reasonability. Restatement (Third) of Property: Servitudes § 3.6 comment b (Tentative Draft No. 2, 1991). See, as examples, of the application of restrictive covenants: *Webster* v. *Star Distrib. Co.,* 241 Ga. 270, 272, 244 S.E.2d 826 (1978); *Hall* v. *American Oil Co.,* 504 S.W.2d 313, 318-319 (Mo.Ct.App.1973); *Davidson Bros.* v. *D. Katz & Sons, Inc.,* 121 N.J. 196, 198, 210-212, 579 A.2d 288 (1990); *Vermont Natl. Bank* v. *Chittenden Trust Co.,* 143 Vt. 257, 261-262, 465 A.2d 284 (1983). Cf. *Jetro Cash & Carry Enterprises, Inc.* v. *Food Distrib. Center,* 569 F.Supp. 1404, 1415-1416 (E.D.Pa.1983). The purpose here is limited, the geographic area is compact, and the duration at this juncture is not inconsistent with the useful life of buildings.

Mobil looks to *Garland* v. *Rosenshein,* 420 Mass. 319, 321 (1995), as a source of support for not enforcing the restriction, but that case gives Mobil no help. In Garland, the only value of the restriction to the person attempting to enforce it was the "hold-up price," i.e., what somebody might be willing to pay to secure release of the restriction. The restriction was not of any use to the party attempting to enforce it in terms of any business that party was carrying on or any real estate development project that party was undertaking or contemplating. By contrast, in the case before us, the restriction against food sales on the gas station site is of current utility to the party that owns the restaurant site. For a somewhat similar restriction in a lease, see *Kobayashi* v. *Orion Ventures, Inc.*, 42 Mass. App. Ct. 492 (1997).

2. Is the restriction unenforceable because it is obsolete? The judge found that the trend in the operation of highway automobile service stations was to integrate into them a convenience store at which a large number of items that might attract drivers were for sale and that, to that degree, a restriction limiting service stations to selling food by vending machine was obsolete. One may well question that conclusion of obsolescence—it is more a conclusion of law than a finding of fact—because the abandonment of machine vending by the gas station operators does not make that limitation at all obsolete to the competing restaurateur. Customers cannot touch and feel a product inside a vending machine and they need the right coins or bills to feed into the machine. Such limitations favor the victualer who deals over the counter, and the proprietor of the restaurants on the Exit 1 land is entitled to resist a metamorphosis of a machine vending operation into a more competitive operation, even if that reflects a more up-to-date service station.

We need neither belabor nor answer the question of the obsolescence of the restriction to vending machine sales because Exit 1 accepts the nature and scale of operations at the gas station site as it was in 1990, and, more specifically, accepts the scale of operations that the judge allowed Mobil in his order:

"[S]ale of food and beverages, as follows: soft drinks and juices and similar bottle beverages in two (2) reach-in coolers, a milk cooler, an ice cream freezer chest, a coffee maker and containers, a display of packaged pastries, chips, peanuts, crackers, candy and other 'snacks', and the beverages packaged in containers such as bottles or cans for sale outside the coolers, and the displays of product for sale shall be limited to the approximate volume which existed in 1990 and shall be further limited to the sale of such products which are packaged by the manufacturer and intended for off-premises consumption."

Mobil argues that once the trial judge found a part of the restriction obsolete, he was bound by G.L. c. 184, § 30, to limit Exit 1's remedy to money damages. The basis of that contention is a clause in § 30, as inserted by St.1961, c. 448, § 1, that reads:

"No restriction determined to be of such benefit shall be enforced or declared to be enforceable, except in appropriate cases by award of money damages, if (1) changes in the character of the properties affected ... or in any other conditions or circumstances, reduce materially the need for the restriction or the likelihood of the restriction accomplishing its original purposes or render it obsolete or inequitable to enforce except by award of money damages."

The judge, however, as we have observed, found considerable pertinence in the original purpose of the restriction. The "need for the restriction," therefore, had not been materially reduced. Contrast *Blakeley* v. *Gorin*, 365 Mass. 590, 602 (1974), in which restrictions on the depth of cellar holes or the erection of stables in the Back Bay section of Boston in the 1970's were understandably determined to be obsolete — although a restriction against mercantile use was not. Assuming, for discussion purposes, a legally sound basis for judging the vending machine component of the restriction to be obsolete, a court may, in enforcing a restriction on competition, adjust the restriction to make it reasonable in the circumstances of the parties at the time they bring the question before the court. See *All Stainless, Inc.* v. *Colby*, 364 Mass. 773, 778, 308 (1974); *Kroeger* v. *Stop & Shop Co.*, 13 Mass. App. Ct. 310, 317-318 (1982). As an example of considerable judicial editing of a restrictive covenant arising out of an employment agreement, see *Wrentham Co.* v. *Cann*, 345 Mass. 737, 742-743 (1963).

3. Laches. There is nothing to the argument that Exit 1 was bound by laches to give up the right to enforce the restrictive covenant. Exit 1 made known in 1990 that it would tolerate some overflow (of competition) into its line of business, but not a flood. *Contrast Myers* v. *Salin*, 13 Mass. App. Ct. 127, 138-141 (1982).

Judgment affirmed.

WILLARD S. LEVINGS, trustee *v.* FORBES & WALLACE, INC.

8 Mass. App. Ct. 498

Middlesex. September 7, 1979 – October 24, 1979

Present: HALE, C.J., GRANT, KASS, JJ.

CIVIL ACTION commenced in the Superior Court on July 8, 1974.

The case was heard on a master's report by *Cratsley*, J., a District Court judge sitting under statutory authority.

Donald N. Sweeney for the plaintiff.

William K. Danaher, Jr., for the defendant.

KASS, J.

Although the underlying cause is a contract action for material sold and services delivered, the insertion in the complaint of a claim under G.L. c. 93A, § 11, requires consideration once again of the reach of that statutory provision to commercial disputes between business organizations.

First, however, we must meet a procedural issue. The complaint was filed on July 8, 1974. It alleged that the plaintiff (Trane), at the request of the defendant (Forbes), repaired a central air conditioning unit located in a department store in Springfield; that Forbes had refused to pay Trane's bill for labor and materials; and that Forbes, from the time it first placed the written order for the work, never intended to pay Trane for its labor and materials. It is the last allegation, that in effect Forbes duped Trane into working for it, on which the c. 93A claim rests.

Procedural skirmishes followed, largely involving efforts by Trane to obtain discovery, which Forbes resisted by leading Trane a merry chase. For this Forbes incurred mild sanctions. Mass.R.Civ.P. 37, 365 Mass. 797 (1974). On March 16, 1976, Trane moved for a speedy trial, and that

71

motion was allowed. On July 22, 1976, however, the case was dispatched to a master on an order of reference which directed him not to report the evidence since Forbes had demanded a jury; i.e., the master was to make his report "facts not final." Not until March 11, 1977, just five days short of a full year after the motion for a speedy trial had been allowed, did the master file his report. Regrettably, this was characteristic of the long and dilatory course of the litigation. The master made findings favorable to Trane, including a finding that when Forbes issued its purchase order to Trane, "it intended not to pay the plaintiff for the work which the plaintiff was to perform pursuant to the purchase order." Forbes filed objections to the master's report, but made no effort to have those objections heard, nor does the record disclose what the objections were. Trane, for its part, never moved for adoption of the report. While the master's report remained in this limbo, Forbes yielded on the contract claim and agreed to pay Trane the full amount of its bill, plus interest.

Trane pressed the c. 93A complaint, which was tried in October of 1977, without a jury since, at that time, an action under c. 93A, § 11, was an equitable action.[1] It is the position of Trane that once the matter became jury waived, the status of the master's report became governed by Mass.R.Civ.P. 53(e)(2), as amended, 367 Mass. 917 (1975), under which the court shall accept the master's findings of fact unless clearly erroneous. If so regarded, the master's report served to equip Trane with the substantial advantage of the master's finding that Forbes hired Trane, never intending to pay for the latter's work. If the master's report is to be regarded as "facts not final," in accordance with the original order of reference, the status of the master's findings is no more than prima facie evidence of the matters found. Prior to the adoption of the Massachusetts Rules of Civil Procedure in 1974, the waiver of a jury trial did not alter the status of a master's (then an auditor's) report. *Ott* v. *Comeau*, 297 Mass. 108, 110 (1937). Under the present rules the view appears to be that "if the master has heard the case 'facts not final,' the principles governing a master's report in a jury case control." Smith Zobel, Rules Practice §§ 53.11 and 53.12 (1977). So to regard the master's report is a particularly apt result in the instant case, where that report

---

[1] Since the instant case was tried before the enactment of St. 1978, c. 478, § 48, we need not decide whether that statute altered the purely "equitable" character of c. 93A actions.

was never adopted and where the parties proceeded without express objection to a full trial (including the testimony of witnesses and the admission in evidence of many exhibits) of the c. 93A issue.

We turn now to whether Trane's complaint stated a case within the scope of c. 93A. As originally enacted, c. 93A undertook to provide" a more equitable balance in the relationship of consumers[2] to persons conducting business activity." *Commonwealth* v. *DeCotis*, 366 Mass. 234, 238 (1974). See also *Tober Foreign Motors, Inc.* v. *Reiter Oldsmobile, Inc.*, 376 Mass. 313, 319 (1978); Alperin Chase, Consumer Rights and Remedies § 123, n. 25 (1979). Complaints brought by consumers had to filter through the Attorney General, who alone could bring enforcement actions. Passage of St. 1969, c. 690, inserted a private remedy provision in the statutory scheme. This appears as § 9. For a review of the history of these developments see *Slaney* v. *Westwood Auto, Inc.*, 366 Mass. 688, 693-700 (1975).

The right to employ the potent weaponry of c. 93A (new substantive rights, multiple damages, counsel fees) was conferred upon businessmen,[3] as opposed to consumers, by St. 1972, c. 614, § 2, which inserted c. 93A, § 11, into the General Laws. It is the position of the defendant Forbes that, in a controversy between businesses, the unfair method of competition or unfair or deceptive act or practice of which the injured party complains must (a) have an anticompetitive effect and (b) involve a plaintiff who is a "consumer," i.e., is a vendee or lessee of goods, services or property. In the instant case, the plaintiff Trane was a purveyor of services, rather than a purchaser.

A statement issued by the House Committee on Banks and Banking, which reported favorably on the bill which became St. 1972, c. 614,[4] lends some support to the proposition that the target of § 11 is activity which is anticompetitive in purpose or effect. The focus of the House Committee's statement is exclusively on the consequences to consumers and the economy of unfair competition: businesses which could not

---

[2] The statute defined a consumer as "[a]ny person who purchases or leases goods, services or property, real or personal primarily for personal, family or household purposes ..." G.L. c. 93A, § 9(1), as amended through St. 1971, c. 241.

[3] "Any person who engages in the conduct of any trade or commerce ..." G.L. c. 93A, § 11, inserted by St. 1972, c. 614, § 2.

[4] 1972 House Doc. No. 3124.

survive unfair competition would close, allowing the survivors to set higher prices in a monopolistic environment, to the detriment of consumers. The language of § 11 suggests no such limitation, however; it speaks in terms of "an unfair method of competition or an unfair or deceptive act or practice" (emphasis supplied). The disjunctive nature of the wrongs categorized in § 11 comes into sharp relief in *PMP Associates, Inc.* v. *Globe Newspaper Co.*, 366 Mass. 593, 596-598 (1975), in which the court held that a refusal to sell advertising space did not, without more, constitute an unfair trade practice because it was "not within any recognized conception of unfairness, [was] neither immoral, unethical, oppressive nor unscrupulous." *Id.* at 596. Coupled with an anticompetitive motive or effect, the court observed, *id.* at 597 and citing numerous cases arising under the Trade Commission Act,[5] this otherwise innocent practice might well become unlawful under c. 93A. It follows by necessary implication that a business practice which did fall within a class of activity described as unfair or deceptive in *FTC* v. *Sperry Hutchinson Co.*, 405 U.S. 233, 244 (1972), and 29 Fed. Reg. 8325, 8355 (1964), would be proscribed by § 11 and, therefore, actionable without the additional anticompetitive trait. In *Frank J. Linhares Co.* v. *Reliance Ins. Co.*, 4 Mass. App. Ct. 617, 623 (1976), for example, we said that allegation of a refusal to deliver a truck to which the plaintiff had a right of possession unless the plaintiff should agree in writing to release the defendant from warranties or repairs stated a good § 11 claim. The defendant's activity in that case had no anticompetitive overtones.

Forbes' argument that only buyers, not sellers, may avail themselves of remedies under § 11 finds no support in the statutory language or its history. Until recently, G.L. c. 93A, § 9(1), limited rights of action to persons who were purchasers and lessees while § 11, however, contained no such limitation; rather it conferred the businessman's 93A claim on "any person who engages in the conduct of any trade or commerce." The remedies and procedures in §§ 9 and 11 are related, but not parallel, and the conditions of one section should not be read by implication into the other. *Nader* v. *Citron*, 372 Mass. 96, 99-101 (1977). In any event, St. 1979, c. 406, § 1, enacted last July, eliminated the purchaser and lessee qualification from § 9(1). As that provision now reads, "Any

---

[5] 15 U.S.C. § 45 (a) (1) (1976).

person, other than a person entitled to bring action under section eleven ... who has been injured by ... any method, act or practice declared to be unlawful by section two" may bring an action under c. 93A. It does not, incidentally, require an exceptionally lively imagination to conjure circumstances under which an economically powerful business in the capacity of a buyer might act unfairly in relation to a small business in the capacity of a seller of goods or services.

It remains to ask whether, on the facts found, Forbes has committed a transgression which exposes it to a c. 93A claim, i.e., did it do anything unfair or deceptive? What is unfair is a definitional problem of long standing, which statutory draftsmen have prudently avoided. "It is impossible to frame definitions which embrace all unfair practices. There is no limit to human inventiveness in this field." H.R. Conf. Rep. No. 1142, 63d Cong., 2d Sess. (1914). The criteria adopted in our decisions are those spelled out in *PMP Associates, Inc.* v. *Globe Newspaper Co.*, 366 Mass. at 596, and derive in large measure from the Federal Trade Commission Act, 15 U.S.C. § 45 (a) (1) (1976), and regulations thereunder. Those criteria require us in a case such as this to look for conduct which is (1) within "at least the penumbra of some common-law, statutory, or other established concept of unfairness; (2) ... is immoral, unethical, oppressive, or unscrupulous ..." 29 Fed. Reg. 8325, 8355 (1964). Whether a given practice runs afoul of these touchstones must be determined from the circumstances of each case. *Don Lorenz, Inc.* v. *Northampton Natl. Bank*, 6 Mass. App. Ct. 933 (1978). The objectionable conduct must attain a level of rascality that would raise an eyebrow of someone inured to the rough and tumble of the world of commerce. Thus, to refuse to pay for goods or services because one disputed the amount of the bill does not give rise to a c. 93A action. That statute has not superseded the common law of contracts or the Uniform Commercial Code and "not every unlawful act is automatically an unfair (or deceptive) one under G.L. c. 93A." *Mechanics Natl. Bank* v. *Killeen*, 377 Mass. 100, 109 (1979). A misrepresentation in the common law sense would, however, be the basis for a c. 93A claim. If Forbes, therefore, ordered goods and services from Trane and thereby induced Trane to work for it, all the while never intending to pay for that labor and materials, Trane would have a c. 93A action against Forbes.

The trial judge found, however, that no such deceitful intent by

Forbes had been established. Rather, he found that Forbes intended to pay Trane for the reasonable value of the work for which it was obligated to pay. The judge based his finding, among other things, on the fact that the purchase order contained no price and since Forbes offered to pay something more than half the amount of the bill, it might have paid a smaller bill without cavil. The judge also found there existed a bona fide dispute about the scope of the manufacturer's warranty concerning the air conditioning motor. On our review of the record we cannot say the judge was wrong. Accepting the facts found by the judge, there was no misrepresentation by Forbes, and its conduct cannot be said to have fallen to that level which gives rise to a c. 93A action.

Earlier in this opinion we commented on the long and dilatory course of this litigation. On no less than ten occasions in a relatively simple case the defendant caused delay in the proceedings. It answered late; it filed tardy and inadequate answers to interrogatories and only after a court order to do so; it declined to produce documents until on more than one occasion it was ordered to produce them; it moved to continue the master's hearings for a month, and then its lawyer failed to appear for the third session of those hearings (without prior notice to the plaintiff's counsel). A review of the docket discloses six occasions when the intervention of the court was required to secure compliance by the defendant with the discovery process.

Sanctions under Mass.R.Civ.P. 37, 365 Mass. 797 (1974), were imposed on the defendant in two instances: $415 in attorney's fees for failure to comply with an order to produce documents; $150 for failure to answer interrogatories fully. Trane has raised the adequacy of these sanctions on appeal. In isolation, each instance of delay and resistance must have seemed a routine aggravation, insufficient to call down judicial wrath. Collectively, even making due allowance for the plaintiff's procedural aggressiveness, the instances of the defendant's lack of conscientiousness in making discovery (and delaying the orderly progress of the litigation) represent abuse to which courts ought not to be subjected. *Partlow* v. *Hertz Corp.*, 370 Mass. 787, 790-791 (1976). See *National Hockey League* v. *Metropolitan Hockey Club, Inc.*, 427 U.S. 639 (1976). Note, The Emerging Deterrence Orientation in the Imposition of Discovery Sanctions, 91 Harv. L. Rev. 1033 (1978). On our view of the record, the sanctions imposed fell far short of the cost to the plaintiff of obtaining discovery. Compare *Henshaw* v. *Travellers Ins. Co.*, 377 Mass. 910 (1979). If in the past rule 37 has been seen as a "paper tiger,"[6] it is not too late to put some teeth in the tiger.

Accordingly, the action is remanded to the Superior Court for review of the orders made in response to the plaintiff's several motions for sanctions, and the modification of those orders in a manner consistent with this opinion. The judgment is otherwise affirmed without costs.

So ordered.

---

[6] Rosenberg, New Philosophy of Sanctions, appearing in New Federal Civil Discovery Rules Sourcebook 140, 141 (Treadwell ed. 1972).

WILLIAM G. BOWERS[1] *v.* BOARD OF APPEALS OF MARSHFIELD & others[2]

16 Mass. App. Ct. 29

Plymouth. March 16, 1983 – May 17, 1983.

Present: ARMSTRONG, KAPLAN, & KASS, JJ.

Further appellate review denied July 1, 1983.

CIVIL ACTION commenced in the Superior Court on July 11, 1977.

A motion to vacate judgment was heard by *Wagner*, J.

Robert L. Marzelli, Town Counsel, Pembroke, for Board of Selectmen of Marshfield.

Justin C. Barton, Norwood, for plaintiffs.

KASS, J.

In 1977, Marshfield, acting through its department of public works, was on the brink of constructing a wastewater treatment plant and appurtenant sewage pumping stations. One of those pumping stations was to be located on Avon Street and in connection with it, the town required from its board of appeals a site plan approval[3] which was in the nature of a special permit.[4] This the board granted, and the plaintiffs, who were abutters to the proposed pumping station, brought an appeal under G.L. c. 40A, § 17.

From the town's point of view, it was necessary to dispose of the challenge to the board of appeals decision with dispatch, or fifteen

---

[1] Jeane Ann Bowers.

[2] Department of public works of Marshfield, superintendent of public works, and the board of selectmen of the town of Marshfield.

[3] Town of Marshfield, Zoning By-law § 12.02.

[4] By-law, § 10.10.

million dollars in Federal and State financial assistance for the overall project would be lost. An attempt to dispose of the matter by summary judgment failed. Faced with the considerable pressure of the loss of funding for the project, the town and the plaintiffs arrived at a deal: the plaintiffs would agree that the board of appeals had acted within its authority; the selectmen of the town would intervene in the action and agree that they would cease using six adjoining lots as a public parking area. The parties drafted an agreement for judgment setting forth the negotiated terms. As to the six lots, the agreement for judgment provided as follows:

"That the defendants are permanently enjoined from using or suffering to be used, directly or indirectly, the following area of land as a parking area: Lots 145, 147, 149, 151, 153 and 155 as shown on the Plan of Land, Duxbury Beach, in Marshfield, Plymouth County, Massachusetts recorded with Plymouth Registry of Deeds in Plan Book 1, Page 149, Serial No. 824."

The parties also agreed to "waive any and all rights of appeal from this judgment."

A District Court judge sitting in the Superior Court by statutory designation entered judgment in accordance with the agreement. The judgment was recorded in the Registry of Deeds for Plymouth County.

The following summer there were several inconclusive procedural maneuvers which it is not necessary to detail, except to observe that they were stimulated by residents of the town aggrieved by the loss of parking which they were accustomed to have available when visiting Green Harbor Beach. Few events so stir the civic consciousness as the removal of convenient parking.

Nothing happened so far as judicial proceedings are concerned until February 16, 1982, when a newly constituted board of selectmen moved to vacate judgment under Mass.R.Civ.P. 60(b)(4), 365 Mass. 829 (1974), either because the judgment was beyond the power of the court to enter under G.L. c. 40A, § 17, or because the court lacked jurisdiction to impose restrictions on the six lots adjoining the site for the pumping station.

More than four years had gone by since the judgment had been entered in 1977. The sewage pumping station had been built. Notwithstanding the powerful interest in finality of judgments, a motion for relief from a judgment which was void from its inception lies without limitation of time. *Bookout* v. *Beck,* 354 F.2d 823, 825 (9th Cir.1965). *Taft* v. *Donellan Jerome, Inc.,* 407 F.2d 807, 808 (7th Cir.1969). *Misco Leasing, Inc.* v. *Vaughn,* 450 F.2d 257, 260 (10th Cir.1971). Smith and Zobel, Rules Practice § 60.11 (1977). 11 Wright and Miller, Federal Practice & Procedure § 2862 (1973). If the judgment is, in fact, void, the court must grant relief. *Jordon* v. *Gilligan,* 500 F.2d 701, 704 (6th Cir.1974), cert. denied, 421 U.S. 991, 95 S.Ct. 1996, 44 L.Ed.2d 481 (1975). *Thomas P. Gonzalez Corp.* v. *Consejo Nacional De Production De Costa Ric*a, 614 F.2d 1247, 1256 (9th Cir.1980*). Covington Indus., Inc.* v. *Resintex, A.G.,* 629 F.2d 730, 733 (2d Cir.1980). Smith and Zobel, *supra.* Wright and Miller, *supra.*

Jurisdiction existed under G.L. c. 40A, § 17, to consider whether the site plan approval granted by the board of appeals was within its authority. There is, therefore, no cause to disturb so much of the judgment as dealt with that issue.

That part of the judgment which deals with the adjoining six lots is more problematic. Although municipalities and landowners may make agreements to resolve a land use dispute, see *Sylvania Elec. Prods., Inc.* v. *Newton,* 344 Mass. 428, 433-436 (1962), courts which sit in review under G.L. c. 40A, § 17, may not modify substantially the relief granted by a board of appeal. *Pendergast* v. *Board of Appeals of Barnstable,* 331 Mass. 555, 556, 558-560 (1954*). Subaru of New England* v. *Board of Appeals of Canton,* 8 Mass. App. Ct. 483, 486 (1979). *Geryk* v. *Zoning Appeals Board of Easthampton,* 8 Mass. App. Ct. 683, 684-685 (1979).

We are faced with the additional difficulty that the perpetual encumbrance imposed upon the six lots by the then selectmen was an action which they were powerless to take. The power to alienate and dispose of real estate lies with the inhabitants of the town acting at town meeting, with certain limited exceptions, not here material, regarding leases. G.L. c. 40, § 3. See *Ballantine* v. *Falmouth,* 363 Mass. 760, 766 (1973); *Dennis* v. *Lighthouse Inn, Inc.,* 6 Mass. App. Ct. 970 (1979).

That the agreed to judgment required the selectmen to do something for which they lacked authority, i.e., to alienate the six lots by encumbering them, does not compel the conclusion that the judgment was void. An erroneous judgment is not a void judgment. *Foltz* v. *St. Louis & S.F. Ry.,* 60 F. 316, 320 (8th Cir.1894). *Lubben* v. *Selective Serv. Sys. Local Bd. No. 27,* 453 F.2d 645, 649 (1st Cir.1972). 11 Wright and Miller §

2862, at 198-200. Compare *New York Trust Co.* v. *Brewster*, 241 Mass. 155, 162 (1922), in which the court, quoting *Leonard* v. *Robbins*, 13 Allen 217, 219 (1866), observed that "no agreement or assent of the parties will enable the court to render a judgment which the law does not warrant." But in those cases the judgment was attacked by timely appeal. A judgment is void if the court from which it issues lacked jurisdiction over the parties, jurisdiction over the subject matter, or failed to provide due process of law. *United States* v. *119.67 Acres of Land*, 663 F.2d 1328, 1331 (5th Cir.1981). 11 Wright and Miller § 2862, at 198-200. All parties here were properly before the court and a settled case is an unlikely candidate for a due process argument. Had any party raised as an issue the power of the selectmen under G.L. c. 40, § 3, to restrict the lots, the subject would have been appropriate for the court to consider. It is not the category of case involved, but the relief granted, which is in error; a judgment flawed in that manner is not susceptible to attack as void. See generally 7 Moore's Federal Practice, par. 60.25 (2d ed. 1982).

Although the selectmen's motion did not invoke it, clause (6) of Mass.R.Civ.P. 60(b), which authorizes relief for "any other reason justifying relief from the operation of the judgment" was an appropriate provision under which to consider vacating the judgment. The moving party's failure to so classify the motion is not dispositive. *King* v. *Allen*, 9 Mass. App. Ct. 821 (1980). *Lubben* v. *Selective Serv. Sys. Local Bd.*, No. 27, 453 F.2d at 648. 7 Moore's Federal Practice, par. 60.27, at 350.

To secure relief under rule 60(b)(6) requires a showing of "extraordinary" circumstances. *Ackermann* v. *United States*, 340 U.S. 193, 202, 71 S.Ct. 209, 213, 95 L.Ed. 207 (1950); *Artco* v. *DiFruscia*, 5 Mass. App. Ct. 513, 517 (1977). If cases are to have finality, the operation of rule 60(b) must receive "extremely meagre scope." *Rinieri* v. *News Syndicate Co.*, 385 F.2d 818, 822 (2d Cir.1967).[5]

What makes the instant case exceptional is that a public authority, the selectmen, offered as their part of an agreement for judgment a restriction that they lacked the power to impose. We do not deprecate consent judgments. They are a useful device to resolve disputes and are as much of an adjudication for purposes of applying the principle of

---

[5] Ordinarily "Rule 60 is to litigation what mouth-to-mouth resuscitation is to first aid: a life-saving treatment, applicable in desperate cases." Smith and Zobel, Rules Practice § 60.1.

judgment preclusion as any other final judgment. *Fishman* v. *Alberts*, 321 Mass. 280, 281-282 (1947). *Nantucket Express Lines, Inc.* v. *Woods Hole, Martha's Vineyard & Nantucket S.S. Authy.*, 350 Mass. 173, 176 (1966). Indeed, "[r]elief from [16 Mass. App. Ct. 34] a judgment may be sought by or on behalf of a person only if the judgment is or purports to be binding on him under the rules of res judicata ...." Restatement (Second) of Judgments § 64 (1982).

There is in an agreement for judgment, however, an element of contract. *Hentschel* v. *Smith*, 278 Minn. 86, 92-93, 153 N.W.2d 199 (1967). *Pollard* v. *Steffens*, 161 Tex. 594, 602, 343 S.W.2d 234 (1961). *Washington Asphalt Co.* v. *Harold Kaeser Co.*, 51 Wash.2d 89, 91, 316 P.2d 126 (1957). Cf. *Medford* v. *Corbett*, 302 Mass. 573, 574-575 (1939). Accordingly, it is in order to apply to a consent judgment made with governmental authority the familiar principle that those who contract with the officers or agents of a governmental agency must, at their peril, "see to it that those officers or agents are acting within the scope of their authority." *Sancta Maria Hosp.* v. *Cambridge*, 369 Mass. 586, 595 (1976). *Adalian Bros.* v. *Boston*, 323 Mass. 629, 632 (1949). *White Constr. Co.* v. *Commonwealth*, 11 Mass. App. Ct. 640, Mass. App. Ct.Adv.Sh. (1981) 699, 707. Were it otherwise public officials could bind their governmental agencies to unlawful conduct by ready acquiescence in an agreement for judgment and, thus, circumvent the restrictions on their powers.[6] The same officials, or as is the case here, their successors, face the dilemma of acting in excess of their powers or exposing themselves to a judgment of contempt. In those unusual circumstances, resort may be had to rule 60(b)(6). *United States* v. *119.67 Acres of Land*, 663 F.2d at 1331. *United States* v. *32.40 Acres of Land*, 614 F.2d 108, 114 (6th Cir.1980). Cf. *United States* v. *Gould*, 301 F.2d 353, 355-357 (5th Cir.1962). Without weakening the force of an agreement for judgment for purposes of res judicata, it is possible in the context of a motion to vacate judgment to take into account that, as a practical matter, when an agreement for judgment is filed, even its significant nuances will not come to the judge's attention.

We conclude that the judge who heard the motion to vacate judgment properly denied relief as to that portion of the judgment

---

[6] There is no suggestion that the judgment in this case was collusive. Most probably, in the exigency of the moment, the inhibition on the selectmen never came to attention.

which dealt with the relief granted by the board of appeals but should have allowed the motion as to the encumbrance placed on the adjoining six lots.

On the sketchy record before us, we do not know whether vacating part of the judgment might disturb obligations which the town had to State and Federal funding sources. We do know, of course, that it induced a change of position on the part of the plaintiffs, i.e. they abandoned their action under G.L. c. 40A. Although we do not require it so to do, the town may wish to consider its obligations to those funding sources and to the plaintiffs. To that end the order vacating the paragraph of the judgment which enjoins the defendants from using or suffering lots 145, 147, 149, 151, 153 and 155 to be used as a parking area is to be stayed until May 30, 1984, to enable the selectmen to insert in the warrant for the next special or annual town meeting an article authorizing the selectmen to impose the restrictions on those six lots to which the predecessors purported to commit the town at the time of the agreement for judgment. See *Harrison* v. *Building Inspector of Braintree*, 350 Mass. 559, 563 (1966). See also *Village on the Hill, Inc.* v. *Massachusetts Turnpike Authy.*, 348 Mass. 107, 119 (1964).

The denial of the motion to vacate judgment is affirmed as to the first and third paragraphs (not counting the introductory two lines as a paragraph) of the judgment and reversed as to the second paragraph. The second paragraph is vacated. The order shall be stayed in accordance with the preceding paragraph of this opinion.

So ordered.

SPINNAKER ISLAND AND YACHT CLUB HOLDING TRUST *v.* BOARD OF ASSESSORS OF HULL

49 Mass. App. Ct. 20

Suffolk. November 16, 1999 – March 23, 2000.

Present: ARMSTRONG, KASS, & RAPOZA, JJ.

APPEAL from a decision of the Appellate Tax Board.

Brian P. Mansfield for the defendant.

Seth H. Emmer (*William DeBear* with him) for the plaintiff.

KASS, J.

This is the first of two cases that consider whether municipalities may tax rights retained by the declarant of a condominium ("developer") to build additional phases of the condominium.[1] Here, the assessors of Hull assessed real estate taxes to Spinnaker Island and Yacht Club Holding Trust ("taxpayer") for fiscal tax years 1996 and 1997, as owner of ten parcels of land ("expansion parcels") on Spinnaker Island.[2] The Appellate Tax Board (board), after proceedings under its formal procedure,[3] decided that the expansion parcels were part of the condominium's common area as defined by G. L. c. 183A, § 1, and as such, were exempt under G. L. c. 183A, § 14, from assessment as separate parcels of real estate.

1. Facts. By master deed dated January 16, 1985, and recorded with

---

[1] The second case, *First Main St. Corp.* v. *Assessors of Acton*, is reported *post* (2000).

[2] Before the developer made it the site of a condominium, Spinnaker Island was known as Hog Island, a less tony address. The developer made a sail out of a hog's ear.

[3] Compare G. L. c. 58A, § 7 (formal procedure), with G. L. c. 58A, § 7A (authorizing informal procedure).

the Plymouth Registry of Deeds, the developer[4] submitted all of Spinnaker Island to the provisions of G. L. c. 183A, the condominium enabling law. See G. L. c. 183A, § 2. The master deed described a condominium consisting of twenty-two units in ten buildings. That was to be Phase I of the condominium.

Under § 6 of the master deed, the declarant reserved the right, at its sole option, to increase the size of the condominium in phases, to a limit of 103 units.[5] Section 7 of the master deed, captioned "phasing lease," speaks of a lease of the land — on which the additional phases are to be built — that the declarant has "entered into," although it neglects to say with whom or how long the lease shall run. Whenever the declarant built an additional phase, the lease automatically terminated as to the land incorporated in the new phase of the condominium. There is no evidence that any "phasing lease" was ever executed and, as we shall see, there is some evidence that it never was. Details of the developer's option to add to the condominium are further set out in § 14 of the master deed, dealing with amendments to that document. Among the limitations that appear in § 14 is that the developer's right to increase the size of the condominium by building additional units expires January 1, 2004.

In 1985, the declarant added twenty-five units to the condominium; in 1986, thirty-three units; and in 1988, four units. There were then eighty-four units in the condominium. For five years the condominium did not grow further; the real estate boom of the late 1980's had run out of steam. On January 20, 1994, the developer[6] assigned all residual development rights to the taxpayer, a nominee trust of which the sole beneficiary was the condominium unit owners' organization (see G. L. c. 183A, § 10), Spinnaker Island and Yacht Club Association. That instrument of assignment, which bore the caption, "Quitclaim Deed,"

---

[4] The declarants of the condominium were Paul R. Townsend, Francine F. Townsend, Mary N. Fazio, trustees of The Sandcastle Associates Trust.

[5] For a collection of authorities concerning the legitimacy of phased condominiums, a "mutation[] which creative real estate lawyers have contrived," *Barclay* v. *DeVeau*, 11 Mass. App. Ct. 236, 247 (Greaney, J., dissenting), S.C., 384 Mass. 676 (1981), see *DiBiase Corp.* v. *Jacobowitz*, 43 Mass. App. Ct. 361, 364 n.5 (1997), S.C., 427 Mass. 1004 (1998).

[6] Through a series of assignments, the development rights had devolved upon Spinnaker Island, Inc.

refers to the phasing lease "to the extent such Phasing Lease is existent," thereby reinforcing doubt that a phasing lease was ever drafted, let alone signed.[7] Six months later, on June 15, 1994, the taxpayer executed and recorded a document by which it relinquished development rights in eight parcels of Spinnaker Island, but retained rights in ten. Those ten parcels make up the expansion parcels that the town has undertaken to tax. At the time the taxpayer reduced its development rights to ten parcels, the unit owners amended the by-laws of their condominium association to provide that the management board of the association could authorize the addition of units to the condominium only with the consent of the holders of at least sixty-seven percent of the beneficial interests in the unit owners' association.

2. *Discussion.* The theory on which the assessors in this case claim to be able to tax the development rights owned by the taxpayer is that those rights were real property. See G. L. c. 59, § 2A(a).[8]

As the assessors see it, the rights appurtenant to the expansion parcels separated them from the common area of the condominium. In view of the real estate labels used by the developer in dealing with the retained development rights, one may imagine why the assessors were tempted to regard those rights as taxable real property. First there was the phasing lease, and second there was the instrument of assignment of development rights to the taxpayer, which was cast in the form of a quitclaim deed and was expressly so captioned.[9] Labels, however, may not camouflage the underlying reality. See *Commonwealth* v. *Beneficial Fin. Co.*, 360 Mass. 188, 292 (1971), cert. denied sub nom. *Farrell* v. *Massachusetts*, 407 U.S. 910, and sub nom. *Beneficial Fin. Co.* v. *Massachusetts*, 407 U.S. 914 (1972); *American Trucking Assn.* v. *Secretary of Admn.*, 415 Mass. 337, 342 n.9 (1993); *Tinkham* v. *Department of Pub. Welfare*, 11 Mass. App. Ct. 505, 512 (1981); *Cumberland Farms, Inc.* v. *Montague Economic Dev. & Ind. Corp.*, 38 Mass. App. Ct. 615, 621 (1995).

---

[7] The Appellate Tax Board remarked in its decision that the assessors had "failed to prove the existence, let alone the terms, of the phasing lease." No phasing lease was offered in evidence.

[8] For a different basis for taxing retained development rights to build future phases of a condominium, see *First Main St. Corp.* v. *Assessors of Acton, post* at 25.

[9] The document conveyed other interests such as easements and building foundations, for which the quitclaim deed form may have been apt.

General Laws c. 59, § 2A(a), as appearing in St. 1979, c. 797, § 11, provides that "[r]eal property for the purpose of taxation shall include all land within the commonwealth and all buildings and other things thereon or affixed thereto …" By the terms of § 1 and schedule A of the master deed, all the land of the island is submitted to the condominium. Under G. L. c. 183A, § 1, the declarant of the condominium could have done no less, as that statute defines "common areas and facilities" of the condominium as including the land on which the condominium buildings are located. We read the statute as referring to the land dedicated to the condominium rather than the footprint of a particular building. Section 4 of the master deed confirms that the common areas and facilities of the condominium shall include "all areas and facilities of the [c]ondominium as are not within a unit of the [c]ondominium."

Once it is recognized that the expansion parcels constitute common area of the condominium, it follows that they are not subject to real estate taxation because G. L. c. 183A, § 14, as appearing in St. 1963, c. 493, § 1, provides that "common areas and facilities … shall not be deemed to be a taxable parcel." This does not mean that the land of a condominium escapes taxation. "Each unit and its interest in the common areas and facilities shall be considered an individual parcel of real estate for the assessment and collection of real estate taxes." Ibid. That is, the assessors may factor common areas and facilities into the value of an individual condominium unit to be taxed but may not tax them separately. If retained condominium development rights are to be taxed, as we shall discuss more fully in the *First Main St. Corp.* case, *post* at 25, the Legislature shall have to act.

As to the phasing lease, apart from its peculiarly ephemeral quality, even had it existed, the arrangement as described did not purport to give possession to another but was a reservation of right to use common land for additional condominium units, the land under which would continue to be common area. See *DiBiase Corp.* v. *Jacobowitz*, 43 Mass. App. Ct. 361, 364-366 (1997), S.C., 427 Mass. 1004 (1998).

Two cases that stand for the proposition that the statute does not preclude establishing nonownership interests in condominium land are not of assistance to the assessors. *Commercial Wharf E. Condominium Assn.* v. *Waterfront Parking Corp.*, 407 Mass. 123, 125 (1990), involved retention by the developer of an easement in a driveway and parking area before declaration of the condominium, i.e., the real estate was withheld from the common area. Similarly, in *Beaconsfield Towne House Condominium Trust* v. *Zussman*, 416 Mass. 505, 506-508 (1993), the execution of a 155-year lease (of twelve parking spaces) executed and recorded prior to the master deed excluded the parking spaces concerned from the common areas and facilities of the condominium. In the instant case, there has been no exclusion of land from the common areas.

By reason of the unambiguous exclusion in G. L. c. 183A, § 14, of common areas from taxation except to condominium unit owners in proportion to their percentage interests, the expansion parcels are not subject, as separate parcels, to real estate taxation. The decision of the Appellate Tax Board is affirmed.

So ordered.

PEGGY LAWTON KITCHENS, INC. *v.* TERENCE M. HOGAN & others[1]

18 Mass. App. Ct. 937

July 25, 1984

Present: ARMSTRONG, CUTTER and KASS, JJ.

Sylvia Katsenes (William A. Katsenes with her) for the defendants.
Mitchell J. Sikora, Jr. (Harold Jacobi, III, with him) for the plaintiff.

RESCRIPT*

Nothing is sacred.[2] We have before us a case of theft of a recipe for baking chocolate chip cookies. The issue is whether the plaintiff, Peggy Lawton Kitchens, Inc. (Kitchens), possessed a protected trade secret.

A Superior Court judge found that Kitchens first added chocolate chip cookies to its line of prepackaged bakery products in 1960. They were an indifferent success. In 1963, Lawton Wolf, a principal officer of Kitchens, mixed the chaff from Walnuts ("nut dust" he called it) in his chocolate chip cookie batter. This, as the judge found, "produced a distinctive flavor. It was an immediate commercial success." Lawton Wolf, in his testimony, described what nut dust did for his cookies in rhapsodic terms: "Miraculous." Sales, he said "took off immediately. It

---

[1] Ruth A. Hogan and Hogie Bear Snacks, Inc.

* We know that Kass is the author of this rescript opinion, not only because of the distinct style, but also because he was identified as author in the Boston Globe. See Joseph M. Harvey, "Cookie company wins all the chips in a recipe suit", Boston Globe, page 17, July 26, 1984.

[2] See *United States* v. *Byrnes*, 644 F.2d 107, 108-109 (2d Cir. 1981).

did to the cookies what butter does to popcorn or salt to a pretzel. It really made the flavor sing."

The judge found that, from the beginning of its use, Kitchens carefully guarded the cookie recipe. One copy of the recipe was locked in an office safe. A duplicate was secured in the desk of William Wolf, Lawton's son. To satisfied customers who asked for the recipe, Kitchens wrote that the formula was a trade secret. For work day use, Kitchens broke down the formula into baking ingredients, small ingredients (e.g., the nut dust), and bulk ingredients. The three components were kept on separate cards which contained gross weights. Even though those cards concealed the true proportions of the ingredients, access to the cards was limited to long-time trusted employees. The defendant Terence Hogan, whose responsibilities at Kitchens were plant and equipment maintenance and safety, was not among those entrusted with the ingredients cards. Hogan, the judge found, had gained access to the cards through a pretext, and after Hogan left Kitchens' employ, a master key, which could open the vault and the office in which William Wolf's desk was located, was found in Hogan's desk.

Hogan and his wife organized a bakery business to sell prepackaged bakery products under the trade name Hogie Bear. Among the first products Hogie Bear made was a chocolate chip cookie. It had the same recipe, including the miraculous nut dust. The judge found that about forty brands of chocolate chip cookies were sold in New England. Except for those made by Kitchens and Hogie Bear, no two are alike. The judge found Hogie Bear's cookie "similar in appearance, color, cell construction, texture, flavor and taste.[3] They are `formulated' in a similar fashion. They are the same."

As to damages, the judge described the evidence as too vague and speculative to support a finding. A judgment was entered enjoining the defendants from making, baking, and selling chocolate chip cookies which use the plaintiff's formula. On the basis of a finding that the defendants had violated G. L. c. 93A, Sections 2 and 11, the judge assessed against the defendants legal fees of $14,771.50 and disbursements of $1,740.38. A further judgment adverse to the

---

[3] Samples were served up as part of the record on appeal. The time consumed by the appellate process caused the cookies to be in a condition which rendered an appellate taste test of dubious utility, if not downright dangerous.

defendants was entered on their counterclaim, which alleged various unfair practices by the plaintiff Kitchens. We affirm.

The judge's findings of fact, of course, shall not be set aside unless clearly erroneous. Mass.R.Civ.P. 52(a), 365 Mass. 816 (1974). *New England Canteen Serv., Inc.* v. *Ashley*, 372 Mass. 671, 675 (1977).

1. Was there a trade secret? No doubt, the basic ingredients, flour, sugar, shortening, chocolate chips, eggs, and salt, would be common to any chocolate chip cookie. The combination in which those ingredients are used, the diameter and thickness of the cookie, and the degree to which it is baked would, however, constitute a formula which its proprietor could protect from infringement by an employee who either gains access to the formula in confidence or by improper means. *Jet Spray Cooler, Inc.* v. *Crampton*, 361 Mass. 835, 840 (1972). *Eastern Marble Prods. Corp.* v. *Roman Marble, Inc.*, 372 Mass. 835, 838-839 (1977). *Jet Spray Cooler, Inc.* v. *Crampton*, 377 Mass. 159, 165-168 (1979). Restatement of Torts Section 757 (1939).[4] In any event, the insertion of the nut dust into the mix served to add that modicum of originality which separates a process from the every day and so characterizes a trade secret. See *Cataphote Corp.* v. *Hudson*, 444 F.2d 1313, 1315-1316 (5th Cir. 1971). See also *Dynamics Research Corp.* v. *Analytic Sciences Corp.*, 9 Mass. App. Ct. 254, 267-268 (1980). Lawton Wolf's testimony that "sales took off immediately" supports a determination that the improved recipe had competitive value so far as Kitchens was concerned.

2. Conduct of the defendants. Once information qualifies as a trade secret, determination of whether the trade secret has been misused steers the inquiry to examining the conduct of the defendant, and the legal character of that conduct, in turn, is much affected by the steps taken by the proprietor of the trade secret to protect it. See *J. T. Healy & Son* v. *James A. Murphy & Son, Inc.*, 357 Mass. 728, 738-739 (1970); *USM Corp.* v. *Marson Fastener Corp.*, 379 Mass. 90, 97-104 (1979), and cases and authorities cited. Here, as we have seen, the holder of the secret took reasonable steps to maintain its mystery and to narrow the circle of those

---

[4] The Restatement (Second) of Torts dropped the general topics of unfair competition and trade regulation, including the specific topic of trade secrets, because they were seen to be a discrete subject of study that should stand independent of a restatement of the law of torts. See Restatement (Second) of Torts, introductory note to Division Nine at 1-3 (1979).

privy to its essentials. *USM Corp.* v. *Marson Fastener Corp., supra,* at 101-103. We do not think that the absence of admonitions about secrecy or the failure to emphasize secrecy in employment contracts (if there were any in this relatively small business) is fatal to the plaintiff. That Hogan brought no experience in volume baking to his employment with Kitchens and that he employed a ruse to examine the ingredients cards and may have helped himself to a look at the formula tucked away in Kitchens' safe or William Wolf's desk are relevant factors. See and compare *Dynamics Research Corp.* v. *Analytic Sciences Corp., supra* at 267-268. Listing of nut meal on the plaintiff's label does not constitute publication of the recipe because it discloses nothing about the proportions in which the ingredients are used, nor does it say what kind of nuts or what part of the nuts imparted special zing to Kitchens' cookies.

3. The length and breadth of the injunction. The injunction against use of the plaintiff's recipe was permanent and without limit as to area. Injunctions of that length and breadth are unusual, but not without precedent. See *Analogic Corp.* v. *Data Translation, Inc.,* 371 Mass. 643, 647 (1976); *Eastern Marble Prods. Corp.* v. *Roman Marble, Inc.,* 372 Mass. at 842. We do not think the judge was bound to calibrate a more precise area and duration for an injunction as limited as the one imposed. It does not drive Hogan or Hogie Bear Snacks, Inc., out of the cookie business; the injunction forbids only use of Kitchens' precise formula. Other recipes — and the evidence included many — are available to Hogie Bear. There is no limitation on Hogie Bear's packaging or marketing methods. See also *Curtiss-Wright Corp.* v. *Edel-Brown Tool & Die Co.,* 381 Mass. 1, 10-11 (1980).

4. Applicability of c. 93A. Hogan argues that remedies under G. L. c. 93A, Section 11, are not available because *Manning* v. *Zuckerman,* 388 Mass. 8, 11-15 (1983), made chapter 93A inapplicable to employee-employer disputes. Hogie Bear Snacks, Inc., of course, was never an employee of Kitchens. Moreover, Hogan's use of Kitchens' trade secret was made when he was no longer an employee of Kitchens. Hogan's argument crumbles.

Judgments affirmed.

Other writings

Saint Joan, *at the Plymouth*

By Rudolph Kass

The Harvard Crimson, September 25, 1951

One playwright after another has taken a whack at writing a play about Joan of Arc but the play by Bernard Shaw currently being produced at the Plymouth is the pick of the basket. Perhaps its appeal lies in that it avoids being a tearjerker, the fault of several Joan plays, and instead works on the emotions in an honest way.

Much of "Saint Joan" is like much of Shaw: lectures amusingly presented in dialogue form. Yet on several occasions he comes up with lines so thrilling, so poetic, that one starts to consider his claims against his self-chosen arch rival in literary history — Shakespeare.

Margaret Webster, who directed this production, made the most of the balance Shaw got into "Saint Joan." She gets the most out of the moments of heroism and beauty. In the episodes of Shavian preaching, especially the conversations between the Earl of Warwick and the Cauchon, the Bishop who tries Joan, she succeeds in keeping it from deteriorating wholly into a panel discussion.

All the acting was highly professional and not much more need be said in praise. Uta Hagen played Joan, the one genuinely difficult role in the script. She had to switch from moods of humble faith to exhilaration to boisterous daring to impishness. She accomplished the switches without ever making them appear in the least unnatural. Shaw, in his stage directions, describes Joan as a coarse, dumpy little peasant and Miss Hagen was quite beautiful but I suppose this shouldn't be held against her. John Buckmaster would have gained my unbridled huzzahs for his performance as the Dauphin had he not spoken in such a distinctly British manner — something incongruous for a French monarch.

Shaw, Miss Webster, and her accomplished company all stumble lamentably in the last act, an epilogue in which Shaw invokes souls of the dead and the alive into a dream sequence, the object of which is to show the audience that the world is still not ready for saints, no matter how much it admires the dead ones. It is as impossible theatrically as the infamous Don Juan in Hell Scene and considering the perfect ways in which the first scene of Act III ends, I can't help regretting that Miss Webster didn't show more restraint than Mr. Shaw.

BRASS TACKS: THE CAMPAIGN

By Rudolph Kass

The Harvard Crimson, November 2, 1950

This [was] the fourth of six articles on the [1950] elections.

The McCarran Act: A Test

During the current congressional campaign scarcely a candidate has neglected an opportunity to accuse his opponent of knowingly or unknowingly lending aid and comfort to the Communists. The Korean War has so increased the sensitivity of United States public opinion to the threat of Communism, the politicians think, that fierce opposition to it will be a better political asset than an admirable home life and advocacy of virtue.

Support or opposition to the McCarran Anti-Communist Law has often been used as a measure of anti-Communist feeling. The few outspoken enemies of the law who are up for office—Helen Gahagen Douglas of California, John Carroll of Colorado, Jacob Javitts of New York, and Herbert Lehman of New York—claim that the McCarran Act has so many weaknesses that it will do the Communists more good than harm. Backers of the Act assert that to oppose it implies weak tolerance of the Communists if not outright sympathy with them.

Since the McCarran Act was passed, it has been dissected and denounced by liberal and conservative publications all over the country. Even the Chicago Tribune wasn't sure it approved. It is the law which nobody wants, yet it passed through the Senate and over a presidential veto by a vote of 77 to 7, one of the largest margins by which a measure has been approved in the Senate, other than a declaration of war.

It passed so easily because the senators thought it would be political suicide to vote against anti-Communist legislation. So strong was this feeling that Hubert Humphrey of [Minnesota] voted for the McCarran bill 24 hours after he said on the Senate floor that "the day S. 4037 passes will prove to be one of the darkest pages in American History."

Omnibus Bill

An amalgam of the Mundt-Nixon, Mundt-Ferguson, McCarran, and Kilgore proposals, the McCarran Act provides for the registration of all Communists and officers of Communist groups. It requires these groups to label all their property and literature "disseminated by a Communist organization." It bars members of such organizations from obtaining passports as well as from working for the government or in defense plants.

It tightens the espionage laws and extends the statute of limitations in spy cases from three to ten years. It sets up a Subversive Control Board to determine which groups are Communist dominated and provides for judicial review of this board's decisions. It gives the government power, in time of emergency, to intern persons suspected of intent to sabotage. It makes changes, designed to keep Communists out of the country, in the immigration and naturalization laws.

Candidates Tread Lightly

Few candidates in the current campaign have dared object to the McCarran Act on the grounds that it violates traditional liberties. This has been the argument of the C.I.O., A.F.L., and civil liberties pressure groups. Senator Herbert H. Lehman, who voted against the McCarran Act is one of the few candidates who has opposed the law on the moral ground that it is excessively repressive. Lehman's reelection, however, is reasonably assured.

If some of the anti-McCarran Act campaigners win, it may convince politicians that voting against anti-Communist legislation isn't suicide. Repeal or drastic amendment of the current law may then become a possibility. If many opponents of the McCarran Act lose, especially so strong a figure as Lehman, the Act will probably remain unchanged.

Mediation Theater

By Rudolph Kass

June 6, 2016

"How many ages hence shall this our lofty scene be acted over in states unborn and accents yet unknown."[1]

Consider these scenes from mediation theater:

Scene 1: The conflict is about major water damage to ten units in a 110-unit condominium caused by a defect in the construction of the building. The unit owners' association has been slow to react. Therefore, the owners have decided to move on their own against the condominium developer who sold them their units; the general contractor who built the condominium; and the architect who designed it.

The parties elect to take a stab at mediating their dispute. At the mediation, the unit owners assert damages of $180,000. The defendants, each of whom has their own counsel, respond that such an amount is vastly overstated. They offer to settle the case at $24,000. There follow three hours of haggling, at the end of which the demand is down to $60,000, and the response is $57,000. Each side proclaims it has now gone as far as it can go. The mediator — gently — points out that the parties are now only $3,000 apart. If they adopt the judgment of Solomon, i.e., a 50-50 split, they will settle the case at $58,500 to be paid to the plaintiffs by the defendants. Instead of hand shaking, heads shake; visages darken.

Scene 2: Pierce and Strong are neighbors in a single-family

---

[1] Shakespeare, *Julius Caesar*, Act III, Scene 1

subdivision. Pierce plants a hedge of arborvitae along the line of a prior planting of low shrubs that appear to mark the boundary between the Pierce and the Strong lots. Twenty-five years later, in connection with putting his house on the market, Strong orders a land survey and learns that the row of arborvitae, for its entire length, is planted three feet on his property.

Armed with his survey, Strong calls on Pierce, shows him the survey, and tells Pierce, politely, that the arborvitae must go. Pierce, in a less polite way, tells Strong he must be out of his mind. Strong shouts, "It's on my land — you're stealing my land!" Pierce responds that the arborvitae have been there for more than 20 years and claims adverse possession.

After consulting with his niece, a lawyer, Strong tells his neighbor, "There's no adverse possession. I gave you permission to plant those trees, but I did not give you permission to steal from my property."

Strong brings a trespass action against Pierce in the Land Court. At a status conference, the Land Court judge suggests that the parties might do well to resolve their dispute through mediation. At mediation Pierce offers $10,000 in compensation. Strong is insulted.

Scene 3: Barbara Bushbee is a manager of human services at 21st Century Breakthroughs, Inc. Earl Mannik, an erratic but brilliant mathematician, makes unwanted advances upon two women is his department. They complain to Bushbee. She sends for Mannik and warns him if there are further such incidents, he'll be fired. Upper management learns about the incident and tells Bushbee that Mannik is one of the company's most valuable employees, and if she makes further threats like that, she will be fired.

Mannik accumulates a sorry record of recidivism, and Bushbee fires him. In turn, 21st Century Breakthroughs, Inc. fires Bushbee. There follows an action by Bushbee against 21st Century for retaliatory discharge. Her complaint says she was wrongfully fired for enforcing 21st Century's internal rules of conduct and she alleges damages of $1,500,000.

In its answer, 21st Century says that Bushbee willfully ignored instructions from higher management and was deservedly fired. The case goes to mediation. In response to Bushbee's $1,500,000 demand,

21st Century offers $50,000. Again, grim visages.

What is acted over in these three scenes, is personal anger: (1) condominium owners living with construction defects 24 hours a day; (2) neighbors at war over a boundary line; and (3) a human resources manager who did her job as she saw it and yet angered management by her contumacious ignoring senior management order.

In disputes between commercial consenting adults, there will certainly be some theater, several hours of it, but thereafter each party will begin to make risk assessments: the likely litigation expenses and the paralyzing effect on each of the parties if the dispute is allowed to fester. In a cost/benefit analysis, the mediator can help.

In cases involving intense anger, can the mediator intervene constructively? Yes, by moving the conversation from the damage done to the possibilities of undoing them. Putting the onus of the solution on a third party has promise of extracting parties from their dug-in positions.

As an example, in the first case the mediator might suggest the parties engage the expertise of an engineer to make realistic estimates of the cost of making necessary repairs and suggest to the defendants that if they split the repair bill, it will cost them a whole lot less than litigating the disputes.

In the second case, to rise above principle: The mediator suggests to each party that it is time to take a deep breath. Yes, the arborvitae do encroach on the Strong's property. The Pierce and Strong families, however, had been cordial neighbors for more than 30 years. Suppose the new lot dividing line were moved back to the arborvitae, and Pierce paid Strong the amount per square foot for vacant land in their neighborhood — the dollar amount to be determined by a real estate broker or appraiser. Each party consults counsel about the expenses of trial. Peace comes into the room. A grumpy peace.

In both Scene 1 and Scene 2, relatively low cost solutions may get parties over their respective humps. Getting parties to yes may not be fast. There is something in the human species that causes parties to stick to their positions because any give will be seen as a sign of weakness. Part of a frozen negotiation posture is a party's — perhaps subliminal — assumption that if they just hang in there, the other partner to the negotiation will cave, even if just a little. If a party is totally unwilling to budge from its initial position, the mediator may fairly ask: " What did you come to mediate?"

The third case is the hardest. Ms. Bushbee will feel not only anger for standing up for principle, but she is worried about unemployment. She had been well paid by 21st Century. It is doubtful that 21st Century will give her a letter of recommendation. In the world of commerce, secrets have a way of getting out: Mr. Mannik's misconduct and Ms. Bushbee not being a "team player."

This is where "vital interests" come in: Bushbee needs some money to tide her over, and 21st Century doesn't want gossip on the street that it has a hostile environment for women. However sore with one another, 21st Century can announce that Ms. Bushbee is departing to pursue other opportunities; pay her a "bonus" of $500,000; and provide letters of recommendation, which the company recalls had been top notch. Bushbee, for her part, agrees to speak no evil of 21st Century.